WHEN
SONS AND
DAUGHTERS
CHOOSE
ALTERNATIVE
LIFESTYLES

WHEN
SONS AND DAUGHTERS CHOOSE ALTERNATIVE LIFESTYLES

Mariana Caplan, M.A.

Hohm Press
Prescott, AZ

Library of Congress Cataloguing-in-Publication Data

Caplan, Mariana, 1969-
   When sons and daughters choose alternative lifestyles / Mariana Caplan.
   p.   cm.
   Includes bibliographical references.
   ISBN 0-934252-69-6 (alk. paper)
    1. Parent and adult child.   2. Audlt children--Family relationships.
   3. Conflict of generations.   4. Life style.   5. Subculture   I. Title.
   HQ755.86.C36   1996
   306.874--dc20   96-13825
                                                 CIP

Cover: Kim Johansen, Black Dog Design
Typesetting and Layout: Word Handlers, Tucson, AZ

Hohm Press
P.O. Box 2501
Prescott, AZ 86302
(520) 778-9189

Disclaimer: No information in this book is intended to be a replacement for psychological counseling or legal counsel. Any person with emotional or psychological difficulties in adjusting to lifestyle choices of others should consult a qualified health professional; persons needing legal advice should seek legal counsel.

For Lee

Acknowledgements

I'd like to extend my profound gratitude to the numerous individuals who opened their hearts and revealed their stories to me in our shared vision that other parents and children in similar situations may be given the knowledge and encouragement to choose Love over personal differences. I'd like to specifically thank Lee Lozowick, who was the source and inspiration for this book; Joan Capellini, whose life and attitudes serve as a model for the possibility presented within these pages; and my editor, Regina Sara Ryan, whose devotion has made this book possible.

Contents

*I*ntroduction

When Tom left his Master's degree program in economics at a well-known university, moved to an organic farming community in the countryside and began to eat a strictly vegetarian diet, his parents were bewildered. "He's throwing away his life!" they said, panicked. "How could someone in his right mind make such a choice?" they wondered. They immediately cut off all financial support in the hope that he would recognize the mistakes he had made.

When Kristin broke off her marital engagement, changed her name to *Lakshmi*, and began practicing meditation with a group of spiritual students in the Pacific northwest, her parents were outraged. They thought she had surely been brainwashed by the group's leader, and made plans to have her "kidnapped" from her new community.

When Marc, a successful entrepreneur and prominent member of the local Protestant church, and his wife Mary, a Sunday school teacher, announced to Marc's parents that they had decided not to have children and instead to focus their attention on social justice issues throughout the world, Marc's parents were devastated. Marc's father had counted on Marc to "pass on the family name," and Marc's mother had always longed for grandchildren. They did not understand how he could make such a choice, and felt betrayed by his decision.

When an adult-child chooses to live an alternative lifestyle, it is common for parents to feel afraid, hurt, alarmed and concerned. This is a difficult and challenging situation for most parents to accept. Fortunately, there is hope and there is help. Parents as concerned as you have learned to cope with these choices, and have emerged from this challenge with deeper understanding and stronger relationships with their sons and daughters as a result of having gone through this.

I do not purport to be an expert on cult psychology, nor an authority on alternative communities. Nonetheless, as a writer and therapist, and as someone who has lived in many different cultures and struggled with the issues of alternative lifestyle and relationship in my own life, I have come to understand the concerns and pain that both parents and adult-children are confronted with when facing these issues. I have counseled and extensively interviewed those who have chosen to live a vast array of lifestyles, as well as the parents of these individuals who are struggling to understand and accept those choices. I have met with parents who have completely alienated their sons and daughters, as well as those who have come to fully embrace their son's or daughter's choice of lifestyle. In doing so, I have come to recognize the vast range of reactions that parents have when finding out about their son's and daughter's lifestyle choice, and numerous factors that contribute to parents' responses. I have seen clearly that it is not the situation itself that is responsible for the success or failure of the relationship between parents and their adult-children, but rather, it is a shared willingness to have a genuinely loving and respectful relationship between them that is the determining factor.

What This Book is Not

This book is not a manual on how to rescue your son or daughter from any type of community, cult, religious sect, or other form of alternative lifestyle. This book will not provide lists of "good cults" versus "bad cults," or give extensive guidelines for assessing your adult-child's situation. This book will not tell you how to approach having your son or daughter "kidnapped" or "deprogrammed," nor will it advocate approaching him/her in ways that would be perceived as aggressive. This book will not lump all life choices that are not "mainstream" into the category of "cult," as the mass media so often does, and thereby proceed to provide blanket statements about how those who participate in groups should be dealt with.

This book will not support any type of activity that will result in alienating, shaming, criticizing, or diminishing the uniqueness of your adult-child's inherent wisdom and her capacity to make choices that are based in that knowledge. No matter what the perceived goal of the parent's intervention is, this book will not advocate any form of investigation into an adult-child's community or lifestyle that is not the result of direct and honest communication with her. This book will neither state nor imply a distinction between "adult" as wise and knowing, and "child" as naive and ignorant — particularly when that child is now an adult. This book will not support those forms of communication and interaction that will in any way diminish the integrity of either the parent or the adult-child. In essence, this book will not support anything that does not support relationship — nurturing, respectful, gentle, compassionate, loving relationship.

What This Book Is

This book is a manual that will help guide a parent in bridging the gap of alienation and separation with his or her son or daughter when that son or daughter chooses to live an alternative lifestyle. Whereas popular cult literature examines these issues from the perspective of a problem that must be solved, the context for this book is one of the need for parents and their adult-children to maintain relationships that honor and respect people *as they are,* irrespective of any ideological differences or lifestyle choices that either may uphold. Furthermore, this book is based on the understanding that the diversity of alternative lifestyles available, and the variety of ways to relate to these groups, are as numerous as the individuals who are involved in them. In other words, every situation is unique.

Step by step, this book will assist parents in navigating through what may be the initial storms of pain and turbulence, diving into the depths of understanding the alienation that may be felt between them and their sons or daughters, and eventually emerging into the clear waters of effective and practical ways of supporting and being in relationship. This book will give attention to the simple, practical and necessary concerns and processes that parents often go through in their struggle to come to an understanding and acceptance of their adult-child. Though there are no short-cuts to this process, as parents move through these phases, their actions can gradually come to be a reflection of their wisdom and understanding, instead of a manifestation of outdated and unconscious ways of relating to their son or daughter.

A Call to Sanity

This is not a self-help book in the ordinary sense of the word, though by deeply considering and enacting the approaches presented in this book, you will be helped. In fact, you may experience profound changes in relationship not only to your son or daughter, but also to yourself. Rather, this book is a call to sanity in relationships. There is a desperate need to create sane, loving, and harmonious relationships; an imminent need for children, and not only your children but all children, to be raised in environments that truly support who they are. The world *needs* role-models of parents who are wise in their love and in their actions. Admittedly, this is not easy for anyone to do, but certainly worth attempting. The creation of a respectful and harmonious relationship with your son or daughter is simply one milestone on a much larger road.

Most people want to make a difference. Most people desire to contribute something to the world. However, there is a tendency to think that one must do something *large* or *great* in order to accomplish this. This book proposes that in a time of widespread disharmony, war and unstable families; in a time where the word "abuse" has become a part of everyday vocabulary; and in a time when emptiness and depression have become the norm, and fullness and creativity are the exception, that the singular decision to work toward a responsible and loving relationship, particularly with a family member who has made a life choice other than the one which society has slated for him/her, *is* to make a difference.

The Term "Adult-Child"

The term "adult-child" is used is to remind parents that their "children" who have chosen to lead alternative lifestyles are now, in fact, *adults* who are capable of, and must necessarily make, their own life choices. While it is true that in one way, a child will always be a child to his/her parents, this type of sentiment should not be confused with, nor negate the parents' capacity to recognize the time when their child has become an adult, and needs to be allowed to take responsibility for his/her own life.

The "child" who is in fact an "adult" should be acknowledged as such. This recognition alleviates parents from taking responsibility for circumstances that are not in their domain of control, while simultaneously empowering their adult-children to make their own choices reflecting their own integrity.

What is a Cult? What is an Alternative Lifestyle?

The term "cult" has become associated with such tremendous bias in contemporary culture that even the most open-minded of individuals cannot hear the word without having a series of associations triggered in conjunction with it. The dictionary defines the term "cult" as "a system of religious worship." In this context, it is obvious that all major and minor religions, as well as smaller sects and spiritually-based organizations are indeed "cults." Yet it is equally obvious that Catholics, Protestants or Muslims do not consider themselves to be members of cults, nor do they identify with the numerous forms of slander and negativity that are attributed to these organizations.

Society and the mass media have often portrayed "cults" as fanatical organizations run by charismatic leaders who "brainwash" or use "mind-control" to dominate innocent and naive people. Images of hippy communes or collectives in which everybody is running around half-naked and taking drugs are often evoked. Those cults that the media depicts are often the most extreme and violent examples of what can occur in a non-mainstream living situation, yet are often believed to represent all alternative lifestyles. However, the vast majority of alternative lifestyles and communities do not fit into this classification. The media does not portray the hundreds of active alternative groups who are successfully carrying out responsible lives of harmony and integrity.

What then does the term "cult" describe? As Tim Miller states in his article "Cult as a Useless Word": "The fundamental problem here is that the word 'cult' as it is popularly used in the United States, no longer has any descriptive value. It doesn't communicate any clear, focused concept, but rather simply indicates a prejudgment of disapproval."[1]

A concerned individual or a disapproving society can conveniently label any religion or alternative philosophy it does not understand with the term "cult." This safe and uncomplicated classification eliminates the need to consider the specific situation or circumstances involved, and discards the necessity for the individual to face his own fears and biases when confronted with something that he feels averse to or threatened by. However, there is a price to be paid for this convenience. In drawing conclusions based on blanket concepts, the truth of any given situation may be lost. In consciously or unconsciously drawing generic conclusions, the individual cheats himself out of the opportunity to open his mind and to act in accordance with the obvious needs of the moment as opposed to the tendencies of his bias.

Just as the term "cult" does not refer to a specific ideology, philosophy, or set of beliefs, "alternative lifestyle" does not point to any one particular way of life. For our purposes, "alternative lifestyle" will be defined as "any way of life, of a person or group, offering practices or choices that differ from the conventional ones." In this context, the term "alternative lifestyle" neither

---

[1] Reprinted with permission from *Communities Journal of Cooperative Living, Fall*, 1995, 1 yr., $18, sample $5. 138 Twin Oaks Road, Louisa, VA 23093. (540) 894-5126.

includes nor excludes any type of religious or spiritual association. Practically speaking, any group, structure of association or system of belief that differs from the cultural norm could be included in this definition. People who decide to live in a monastery, couples who choose to have no children, single mothers who choose to adopt children, individuals in gay or lesbian relationships, artists who determine to make a living solely from their craft — are all examples of alternative lifestyles.

Because the term "alternative lifestyle" is a relatively new term and does not carry with it the degree of bias that is associated with the term "cult," it is primarily used throughout this book. However, there are points throughout the book when the term "cult" is used, at times interchangeably with the term "alternative lifestyle." This is done, in part, to lessen the charge commonly associated with the term "cult," allowing the word to be utilized in a neutral and unbiased way; and, to give the reader who is convinced that his or her adult-child is involved in a "cult" and who supports the biases that society commonly associates with this, an opportunity to consider this involvement in a slightly different context. This is not to say that there are not alternative and spiritually-orientated groups that present physical and emotional dangers to their members, but instead to remind the reader that just because something is labeled as a "cult" does not imply that danger, mind-control, brainwashing or other forms of coercion and manipulation are present.

As a point of focus, this book specifically references alternative communities and spiritual organizations. However, the principles outlined in the book are applicable to most other circumstances. This book can serve as a guide not only for parents, but also for grandparents, siblings, mates and close friends of a person who has chosen a lifestyle with values that are different from those upheld by society-at-large. These principles can be still further applied to all life transitions, for it is a book about coping, about change, and about moving from shock into acceptance of the circumstances of one's life.

If you jump to the conclusion that because your son or daughter is pursuing an alternative lifestyle he or she is involved in a dangerous cult, you most likely create a lot of unnecessary concern. Coming to understand and respect alternative lifestyles as viable options to mainstream living will widen your perspective on this issue. Doing so will open you up to the possibility for a more loving, compassionate and respectful relationship with your adult-child.

When Your Child is Under 18

If your son or daughter is under eighteen years of age and has chosen to live an alternative lifestyle, you may have particular concerns. Emancipation refers to the age of a child after which parents have no further right to control, nor obligation to support their child. In most states, this age is eighteen years, but it may vary from state-to-state.[2] However, just because your child is under eighteen and living an alternative lifestyle, you should not assume that he is in a dangerous or unhealthy situation; but, it is a good idea for you to have more specific details of his living circumstances when this is the case. You should have the address and phone number where your son or daughter can be reached, and it is not unreasonable to request that he or she contact you on a regular basis to keep you informed of their health and safety.

Besides your legal responsibility to your children, it is likely that you have emotional concerns about their well-being. There are a few things to consider in this domain. It is important to recognize that although to most parents a child is always a child, there is a significant difference between a twelve-year-old and a seventeen-year-old, as well as marked variations in maturity among young adults.

---

[2]Oran, Daniel, *Law Dictionary for Non-Lawyers,* Second Edition, West Publishing Co., 1985, p. 108.

The younger the child, the more you may be needed to take on a role of providing him or her with information. A young woman may not have been thoroughly instructed in general sexual education, including HIV, sexually transmitted diseases, pregnancy and birth control. A young man may be dangerously unaware of the facts about various recreational drugs and their side effects. Your daughter may not have considered what it will be like to re-enter high school in a different grade than her friends if she chooses to take a year off of school, or if she falls behind in her studies. Your son may not have considered the economic consequences in later life if he does not complete his high school education.

However, your child may or may not be open to receiving this information from you — the parent. In your concern and anxiety, you may not be the best one to attempt to communicate with your son or daughter in an objective manner. At this point, it may be useful to involve a third party — not to avoid the need for direct, personal contact, but instead to bring greater clarity to your communication. It is essential that this third party be someone whom your child knows and trusts. If your child wants to know if you asked this person to intervene, you should be honest about this. If you are not straight with your kids, you may lose them.

Furthermore, be attentive to *how* you talk to your child. If you speak in a condescending or critical manner, or as if your child was a six year-old, you convey a lack of respect which is likely to result in your pre-teen or teenage child feeling alienated and disregarded.

Most important, keep an open door. (This concept is discussed in depth in Chapter 9 — *How To Support When You Don"t Agree.*) When your child is under eighteen, "keeping an open door" means letting your children know that they can come back to your home at any time, and that they won't "lose face" in the family, or be questioned, blamed, shamed or criticized for their explorations of another lifestyle. You can convey this to them both in words, and also by not being negative and judgmental toward them in your own mind and heart. Your children are doing what they are doing for a reason, and although you might not know what that reason is, you can keep reminding yourself that they are struggling right alongside with you, and that beneath any rebellion or difficulty in your interactions with one another, they want relationship as much as you do. As one young woman writes:

> "Although my mother misses me, she has always known that one day she would have to let me go and let me follow my heart. . . She's still scared, but she speaks to me about the things that she's afraid of in order to learn more about them. Her tone is never accusing, and because of this I want to help her to understand me better."

I. The Beginning — Coping

The initial phase of learning about an adult-child's choice to lead an alternative lifestyle is marked by simply learning to cope with the new set of circumstances. This is the time when parents may have to deal with feelings of shock and loss, while simultaneously making the choice to relate with their adult-child based on their underlying love and respect for him or her as an individual.

1.

Relationship is Everything

Bill was disturbed as he saw his son, Daniel, becoming more and more deeply immersed in a new community. Daniel had just graduated from college with a degree in philosophy, had travelled around the world and was destined to become a university professor. Instead, he was tending to the solar greenhouse and baking bread for the community. All of the discussions they had about Daniel's choices would end up being righteous and cutting debates, and would result in both him and his father feeling terrible. In Daniel's mind, his father was rigid and close-minded; in Bill's mind, Daniel was overly zealous and naive. Nonetheless, both were committed to relationship, and so they began to write ten and twenty page letters to one another. Although these letters were initially heated and critical, each felt that he could be more specific and clear about what he wanted to communicate by putting his thoughts on paper. Throughout a year and a half of exchanging these letters, an understanding and growing sense of compassion began to emerge between them. In retrospect, both Daniel and Bill agree that what transpired through their struggle together was invaluable and that they came to know one another more honestly and more intimately — in a way that would not have happened otherwise.

Relationship is everything. It is the beginning, middle and end of the road. It is the vehicle, the means and the destination. Without relationship we have nothing, and without relationship we are no one. All riches and successes are experienced as essentially meaningless without people to share them with. Wisdom is useless if it cannot be conveyed, and love is incomplete when it is not shared.

As the parent, sibling, grandparent or friend of the individual who has chosen to live an alternative lifestyle, you may experience intense feelings of frustration, concern and betrayal; however, when it comes down to it, it is only the love that exists between you that is of any real value, and that holds any possibility of fulfillment and joy in your lives together. No matter how difficult the struggle, or how upset you may be, holding on to opinions and excessive worry will only result in a build up of resentment and an eventual alienation between the two of you. There comes a point when you may simply need to give in to relationship — to listen, to compromise and to make the necessary sacrifices in order to maintain a loving rapport with one another. It is always worth it; what is sacrificed is minor compared to what is gained. Therefore, this book sets forth the issue of relationship itself, prior to a discussion of the specific details of an adult-child's choice to live an alternative lifestyle. Relationship is the foundation upon which anything meaningful is based.

People commonly relegate the domain of "relationship" to include only spouses or mates. However, the essential issues of relationship are nowhere more apparent than in the relationship between parents and their adult-children. Because of the intensity of the bond that exists between you, the issues raised by your adult-child's lifestyle choice are often charged and upsetting. But it is equally true that working through these difficulties may result in a significant deepening of the bond that you share.

How Relationship Becomes Endangered

When someone you love or feel responsible for engages in an alternative lifestyle, you may feel threatened. The threat is not literal, of course. Instead, what is threatened is the idea about who this other person is who has made such a sudden change, and who you are in relationship to him or her. You may be reminded that what you assumed to be solid ground beneath your feet is actually shifting sand. This can be both frightening and unsettling. When you feel threatened, a quality of subtle but pervasive fear will often underlie your whole experience. Like an invisible filter that distorts all incoming data through its lens, your perception becomes colored by a shade of this fear, while you may not even know it is there. In the subtle pervasiveness of this fear, relationship is forgotten.

When a member of any species, including a human being, feels threatened, there is an automatic instinct to defend itself. Sometimes this defense is overt, sometimes it is subtle. When an adult-child chooses to live an alternative lifestyle, parents rarely express their defense in the form of physically aggressive acts (although some do have their son or daughter kidnapped and de-programmed). What are actually being threatened are the parents' perceptions, emotions and psychological foundations, and there-fore, the battle which often ensues tends to be played out on the field of relationship. The weapons that parents most commonly employ are emotional threats, ideological arguments and the intellec-tualization of feelings. The ammunition is comprised of domination, persuasion, manipulation and psychological control. Although the battle is engaged on subtle fields, the casualties are real. Again, in the heat of the battle, *relationship is forgotten.* Amid the difficul-ties, when you are able to remember that it is genuine relationship that you desire, and to recognize how arguing and worrying impede that from happening, you will again place relationship in the fore-front of your attention and in doing so you will bring the relation-ship back to life.

Do You Want to Be Right or Do You Want to Be in Relationship?

"From the time I was born I was the 'queen' of my grandfather's world. I was his first and favorite grandchild. All throughout my child-hood and adolescence he showered me with attention, with gifts, with money. Nothing meant more to him than when I would travel to New York City to visit him. We used to go to the Macy's Thanksgiving Day Parade every year, sitting in his office in the Pepsi Cola Building on 5th Avenue as the parade passed by. In my senior year in high school, on that day when I broke the news to him that I was going to enter a Roman Catholic convent (he was a staunch Protestant), he hung up the phone, disowned the family, and *never* contacted us again. We heard from his live-in housekeeper that his life got smaller and smaller after that. He died a sadder and lonelier man than he ever was before."

— Rebecca

Rebecca's grandfather chose to be right instead of being in relationship — at the cost of his family. Everybody wants to be right, and all of the time! (If you think that you don't want to be right, think again.) It's not *wrong* to want to be right, it's simply a tendency of human beings. People have an investment in being right because it makes them feel as though they know what is going on; and it allows them to feel secure — if only momentarily. People want to know the truth and to be in control of their lives, and being right allows them to feel on top of their situation. In actuality, it is not so much that we have a deep desire to be right — instead we want to be *all right*. We want to know that we are worthy, and that our opinions matter.

The problem of needing to be right is that in order to do so, usually somebody else must be wrong, and in the instance of an adult-child choosing to live an alternative lifestyle, if the parent is right you can guess who is wrong! Ironically, a person who genuinely believes that *she* is right is often face-to-face with another person who is equally certain that she is right. Each remains stuck in her own worldview and isolated from the other. In the presence of any type of dynamic, be it subtle or overt, in which an individual is insisting that her opinion, belief, ideology, or lifestyle is right, *there is no relationship.* Even if you end up right, you end up alone.

The issues that arise when an individual chooses to live an alternative lifestyle are particularly charged. They lend themselves toward an easy polarization. People want to be right about which movie is good, and what flavor of ice cream is tastiest. But more, they want to be right about their morals, their religion, their philosophy about life, and their political and social opinions.

Yet, as much as people want to be right, they simultaneously crave relationship — they want family! Underneath any number of fears, concerns or emotions, members of a family need each other. In fact, the reason many parents insist about the "rightness" of their perspective about their son's or daughter's lifestyle is that they are afraid. Parents fear that the adult-child's choice will separate them. However, parents may fail to realize that if this separation occurs, it may actually reflect that this relationship was not solid to begin with. When this becomes clear, or parents make a choice to prioritize the relationship with their son or daughter above and beyond the realm of ideas or beliefs, they will simply let go of the need to be right. Such parents will acknowledge that their adult-child's point of view is equally right.

Asking the question, "Do I want to be right or do I want to be in relationship?" is a vehicle to bring what is most essential back home. Few family members really want to be right to the exclusion of being in relationship; when immersed in the strong pull of fear and uncertainty, however, it is easy to forget what we really want. Deep inside, we know that we are still family and that *relationship* is the only choice worth making.

Relationship is Change

Relationship means change. Not only *do* relationships change, but relationship *is* change itself. It is not a stagnant entity, rather it is a process. People tend to think of relationship as something that belongs to them or that can be owned, i.e., "*My* relationship with my wife," or, "*My* relationship with my child." While the wish to own one's children, wife or husband is not necessarily conscious, out of a wish for security the individual often unconsciously creates a long list of unspoken agreements with his or her loved ones. These agreements attempt to solidify the relationship in terms of who is in control, i.e., who "owns" who. Yet, the possibility of truly owning another is like trying to own a given quantity of air, a wild animal, or an ocean. It cannot be done.

Often, one individual will succeed in gaining consent to these unconscious agreements, for the other shares equally in the wish for security. When that happens, people may live together for years with their children and mates in a semblance of harmony. However, these agreements are in no way foolproof, and can be undermined at any moment. The "security" of such a relationship may be threatened by a persistent nagging inside one of the individuals. He or she may not be able to be articulate this nagging, which is really the monotony and limitations of a relationship that is founded on false grounds. When the nagging gets strong enough, one member of the relationship begins to express this dissatisfaction, and from there the relationship slowly crumbles. Another way that this security is threatened is when a son or daughter chooses to live an alternative lifestyle.

No matter how stable and secure any relationship may seem, and no matter how predictable one's spouse or adult-child may appear to be, sooner or later all relationships will transform — people grow up and grow old, move away, change jobs, get married, get sick, die, grow more joyfully in love or lose their vitality, respect and aliveness with one another. To be open to change as it presents itself, instead of waiting for circumstance to place it on one's doorstep, implies both vulnerability and risk. Yet it is essentially the only way to maintain peace in one's relationships. In reality, when you open yourself up to the constantly changing nature of relationship, you cannot go wrong, for there will no longer be stagnancy and "stuck-ness" in your relationships. Only by recognizing that relationship is change — that relationships will and must change and that they cannot be categorized or clung to by fixed ideas about "how it should be" — will parents be able to flow with the inevitable transitions that will occur in their relationships with their sons and daughters.

Relationship is Art

Relationship is art. When you first learn about your adult-child's choice to live an alternative lifestyle, you may simply feel that the relationship between you has crumbled or collapsed. In the initial phases of coping with the transition, your relationship may appear to you to be a mass of frustration and ugliness; anything *but* art! This is not unlike the way a beginning artist feels when he or she first picks up a paintbrush with the idea of creating a vast mural. Nonetheless, there is an art to relationship, and as you eventually become skilled in this art, and begin to immerse yourself in the process of creating a relationship that expresses the truth of your feelings toward your adult-child, you will begin to experience the satisfaction of creativity.

This doesn't always come easily, however. Just as the painter may go through endless hours of frustration, and countless canvasses and colors in order to create a work of beauty, so may you and your adult-child struggle through the periods of misunderstanding, confusion and creative tension that are necessary in order to create a relationship that is beautiful at its core. Know that it is in these difficult hours — when it seems as though your relationship is going nowhere and all you can do is be patient, wait and trust — that the makings of a relationship of depth and substance are being formed.

Relationship is art in motion, an ongoing creative process. Appreciating this *process* can alleviate the anxiety you may feel when you see the situation with your adult-child as a problem that must be solved, or an obstacle that must be overcome. As with the artist, the ability is within you to trust that, by staying committed to your relationship with your son or daughter, continually examining it from various angles and refining it when necessary, you will create something of true and lasting value.

A New Relationship

This book proposes the possibility of a new or renewed relationship. It is not that you must give up your prior relationship with your son or daughter. The "new" relationship may contain many of the same elements that the old one did — you may still share an interest in movies, food, sports or whatever it is that you have enjoyed together in the past. However, the relationship will be new because the foundation of your relationship will change. The quality of your attention in your interactions with your adult-child will be sharper and you will have a greater awareness of the motivations behind your actions. There will be greater relaxation in your new relationship to your adult-child, due to your willingness to trust your son's or daughter's wisdom and maturity. The love that is expressed between you will be more genuine and free of guilt-based sentiment.

Be warned, though, the results of this new way of relating with your adult-child may not turn out to be quite what you expect! Your new relationship is likely to feel uncomfortable, perhaps even *very* uncomfortable, at first. This is *not* an indication that there is anything wrong with your new approach. Instead, the discomfort you experience is precisely because the relationship is new. In many ways it is not different than what you might feel on a first date or at a new job. It is easy for parents to say that they want to have a new relationship with their son or daughter, but to make a break from the old and familiar patterns into the new and unknown is not always easy.

People tend to act in habitual and routine ways in relationship (even if these routines are not effective) instead of attempting something new. In ordinary circumstances, this habitual behavior may have few negative consequences. However, a problem arises when the situation demands a new response but the individual is unable or unwilling to make the changes necessary to meet the present need. This is often the case for a parent when a son or daughter chooses to live an alternative lifestyle — the adult-child may be thinking, acting or relating to the parent in such a way that the parent's *ordinary* response is simply inappropriate.

Although it may be frightening to relate to your son or daughter in ways that you never have before, the possibilities inherent in this new relationship are enormous. You may experience a freedom in relationship to your adult-child that you have never felt before. You may begin to live as "bonded" adults, with qualities of respect and interest that are not usually present between adult and child. There may be an openness in your relationship that will allow you to learn from one another, instead of draining one another; to grow with one another, rather than using your relationship to fill an empty space. You will be *living* a new relationship, instead of clinging to an old and outdated one.

Unconditional Love: Relationship is Not 50% – 50%, It's 100% – 100%

"I had been away for five years — all of which were very turbulent times in relationship to my parents. One day, I decided to do something I had not done for many years. With trepidation, I called up my mother. As soon as I heard her voice on the other end of the line, I said to her, 'Mom, I love you.' There was a shocked silence on the other end of the line, followed by a hasty and awkward response of her returning her love to me . . . Then suddenly there was the sound of her sobs. We still loved each other so much."

We have been taught that relationship is a 50% - 50% deal and that it is a process of give and take. For many parents and adult-children (and all people in fact), to simply relate to one another without argument or subtle criticism, maintaining an attitude of honor and respect, is an excellent first step. Nonetheless, it is useful to recognize and reflect upon a higher potential — unconditional love.

Unconditional love is the ideal. Although there is love in most people's lives, learning to love another person unconditionally is like learning how to walk all over again. Unconditional love is not a codependent-based acceptance, it is a choice to serve another person completely, and to attend to the other with a recognition of his or her highest potential. With unconditional love, the relationship becomes a 100% - 100% agreement, in which each individual focuses entirely on giving and serving the other.

Love that is truly unconditional is given without selfishness, such as immediately attending to the needs of your young child, even when they seem petty and it is inconvenient for you to do so; it means taking out the garbage simply because it is full, even when you know it is not your turn; it means taking the time to listen to what another person is trying to tell you, even when you are not interested and are convinced that his or her opinion is incorrect. Unconditional love is simple — it is the choice to give for the sake of giving, and not for what you will get in return — however, it may be the hardest choice you ever make.

How does one go about making the choice to love unconditionally? You begin by being willing to be honest with yourself and to look closely at your life. You then start to notice the ways that you *do not* feel and act lovingly. When you initially begin to see this, you may feel discouraged for a time, but eventually you realize that you are not alone. Most human beings have never learned to truly love; it is necessary to comprehend this before you can change. At some point you are likely to begin to feel a wish, a need, or a longing for unselfish love to pervade your life. As this longing persists you will begin to find small ways in which you could act more lovingly. As you begin to actually *do* these things, more opportunities to express such love are revealed to you. In time a greater love will begin to surface in your life. You learn to grow love within yourself.

The process of creating and recreating relationship is never ending. Seeing relationship as the hub around which everything in your life revolves can serve as a reference point for you when smaller, but seemingly more imminent concerns arise. When you initially find out about your adult-child's choice to live an alternative lifestyle, amid the often difficult reactions you may be experiencing, it is helpful to remind yourself as often as you can that it is your relationship to your son or daughter that matters most. You are still family. When the difficulties lessen or subside and you adjust to the new circumstances, it will be your ability to relate to your adult-child in spite of the circumstances that will be of value.

2.

When You First Find Out

When you initially find out that your son or daughter, sibling, grandchild or friend has chosen to lead an alternative lifestyle, take a deep breath. Although you may be quite alarmed and worried, experience teaches that most situations of this kind are not nearly as bad as you first imagine. Your shock and uncertainty are probably coloring your vision, and painting a picture that does not match the reality of the situation. Remember, you have weathered many storms prior to this one. Your loved one too will weather the storms in his or her life and make positive life choices that are ultimately in his or her best interest.

10 Steps to An Easeful Relationship With Your Adult–Child

Step #1 — Don't Panic!

"I grew up in a standard, middle-class community in New Jersey where everyone was either Protestant or Jewish. My parents were totally unfamiliar with any type of social or spiritual life outside of the Judeo-Christian standards, so when I joined an alternative spiritual community, they totally 'freaked out.' They didn't understand anything — it was just foreign to them. They said that they were scared, and that the more I talked about how excited I was to be in the community, the more frightened they became. They didn't have any kind of educational background to understand what I was doing other than what they had heard about the Hare Krishna's or the Moonies, and

everything they had heard was very negative, so
they thought I was going to go to hell or something — that they completely disowned me out
of both of their wills."

Don't panic! When parents initially find out about their
adult-child's choice to lead an alternative lifestyle they commonly
find themselves in a frenzy. They lose a sense of clarity and prac-
ticality about how to deal with the situation. Whatever the scenario,
there is rarely an imminent danger of physical harm to your son or
daughter. Any action you might take out of a state of panic is less
likely to yield the results you desire. The panicked parent rushes
out to hire a detective to check-up on an adult-child's present living
situation; the frantic parent immediately sends books and literature
about dangerous cults to her son or daughter.

If you are feeling panic, or other strong feelings of anxiety,
fear or resentment, it may be useful to intentionally refrain from
engaging your adult-child about his or her lifestyle at this time. If
you can not speak without hurting one another's feelings, this may
be the time to communicate through kind and carefully considered
letters instead. The current intensity and panic will pass, and there
will again be a time in which easeful communication is possible.

Commonly, an adult-child will act in an overly-zealous manner when initially beginning to live an alternative lifestyle. Again,
this is no cause for alarm. He or she may talk in a way that sounds
missionary-like, preachy or dogmatic. It is easy at this point to
make the assumption that your adult-child's over-zealousness is a
reflection of a group that is dogmatic, manipulative, and that seeks
to convert others to its principles. However, zealousness more
often arises when someone is feeling so excited and inspired by
the possibilities that this new life represents, that he or she temporarily neglects the need to be sensitive to others' concerns. Remembering that the cause of your son's or daughter's over-zealousness
is likely to be enthusiasm and excitement may allow you to be
calmer and more patient during this initial period.

"Just after my wife and I joined a new religious group, we went to visit her parents for Thanksgiving. We were young, idealistic, and had a cause. Her mother was asking about the teacher of the group. My wife turned to her and said, 'To me he's like God.' Her mother's face went white. It dawned on me immediately that my wife had made a big mistake. It was the middle of dinner and her mother pushed her chair back from the table and said, 'Jesus is God.' It's twenty years later and we're still in the same community, but neither of us would ever speak like that anymore. It's so important to pay attention to who you're talking to and what they can take."

To whatever extent possible, try to allow time for the situation to unfold. Panic is a manifestation of fear, and whereas it is completely natural that you feel concerned and afraid for your adult-child, if you allow that fear to consume you, you may miss the clarity necessary to respond wisely and compassionately.

Step #2 — Don't Jump to Conclusions

Be careful about the tendency to draw quick conclusions — either about the group your adult-child is involved with, or about your adult-child himself.

If you believe that your adult-child is involved in a cult, whatever you perceive that term to mean, recognize that most of the organizations that are popularly classified as "cults" are not dangerous to your adult-child's physical or emotional well-being. If you have not been exposed to the vast variety of philosophies and living situations that are associated with the terms "cult" or "alternative lifestyle" (and most parents have not), it is inevitable that you would have this fear, for the media portrays a highly biased and distorted view of alternative lifestyles. For sensationalism, newspapers and television depict only the most violent and abusive incidents that occur in alternative living situations, and in doing so convey a message to the public that "this is what happens in cults." Such portrayals do a great disservice to concerned parents, as the vast majority of alternative living situations offer no physical threat to their members, and it is extremely rare for an organization to hold members against their will. If this is your concern, it is particularly important that you not jump to conclusions that will bring unnecessary anxiety to yourself, and undue reactivity in relationship to your adult-child.

It is equally important not to draw conclusions about your adult-child himself. Not only is your son or daughter a unique individual, but whatever has prompted him or her into choosing an alternative lifestyle, how he relates to the particular organization he is involved with, and how he is influenced by his circumstances is *entirely specific to the situation* and to the individual himself. Be careful not to undermine your own sense of your adult-child's inherent intelligence — he has not "become somebody else" overnight. If you have a set of preconceived notions about any given group of people, or about how people involved in this particular group should be dealt with, you handicap your own ability to perceive what is actually happening with your adult-child and how you can be of best use to your son or daughter in the present situation.

"We had a parents' weekend in my community. There was a talk in which the leader was available to talk to the parents about their concerns. My father asked the teacher, 'How do I know if my child will be safe in the community?' One of the children in the community, an eight-year-old girl, turned to me and said, 'Did he just call you a child?' Only an eight-year-old could see how odd it was to call a forty-four-year-old woman a child."

When an adult-child who chooses to live an alternative life-style encounters any natural stresses of life, his or her parents are often tempted to assume that these stresses are the fault of the life-style or the leader of the group in which the adult-child is involved. "If she was leading a more 'normal' lifestyle she would be free of these problems," parents mistakenly assume. For this reason, adult-children often feel as though they must make their life situations sound perfect so that their parents won't jump to conclusions, become more anxious or do something to undermine their relationship further.

> "If I was living in Manhattan and was married with three children, I would be able to call my mother up and tell her that my washing machine was broken, or that one of my children had the flu. I would be able to tell her that I was having difficulties in my relationship with my husband, or that I was concerned that I didn't have enough money. However, because of the lifestyle I lead, everything that isn't perfect in my life tends to alarm my parents. If I don't have enough money, they think that I am not a 'real' professional, or that I am giving all my income to the community. If I am having problems in my relationship, it is because my partner is 'New Agey' and eccentric. They assume that if I was still an uptown accountant that everything would be great."

Realize that the same trials and tribulations that arise in the context of "ordinary lifestyles" will also arise in alternative lifestyles, and that such trials are not indicative of some negative aspect of the alternative situation, but are part and parcel of life itself. When approaching your adult-child about his present lifestyle, attempt to view the situation with "new eyes" — a perspective that will allow you to comprehend the reality of what is going on based on the awareness that each set of circumstances is entirely unique.

Step #3 — Don't Just Do Something, Stand There!

When Ellen received a letter from England from her daughter, Sarah, saying that she was going to leave her job teaching at the elementary school and live with a group of traveling performers, Ellen was alarmed. Although it was the middle of the night in England, Ellen picked up the phone to call her immediately, convinced that she must persuade Sarah out of her choice before her daughter did something she would regret.

To the extent that you are able, don't immediately try to rescue or "save" your son or daughter. First of all, it is unlikely that your adult-child needs to be rescued, and secondly, you cannot save somebody who doesn't want to be saved. It simply won't work.

When people are in pain they just want the pain to go away, and fast. Parents frequently respond to their pain and concern for their sons or daughters by attempting to immediately remedy the situation. They may want to tell their adult-child what they know to get her to see how she is being misled, or to show her how she is betraying her religion, for instance. They want to do something, say something, get somebody else to say something — anything.

Such action, however, is generally an unnecessary over-protectiveness of the adult-child. Whether your attempt to rescue or save your adult-child is conveyed in a way that is caring and considerate, or whether it is expressed in an aggressive and critical manner, the message that is conveyed to your adult-child is: *I know what is best for you better than you do.*

Now may not be the best time to act. Instead, it may be the ideal time to stand still . . . to do your best to put all biases aside and simply listen to your adult-child. The value of listening cannot be understated and will be considered in depth in Chapter 4 — *Approaching Your Son or Daughter.* By listening without reacting, and by being patient, you are communicating to your adult-child that you trust her, that you are interested in understanding her situation, and that you are willing to learn about her new life choice as she feels comfortable sharing it with you.

If you stop, listen and wait, you will notice that your adult-child is looking to see whether or not you will respond in a way that is supportive of *her*, as opposed to her choices. If you wish to provide this kind of support, you must be willing to allow some time and space for your initial reactions to quiet down, to release some of their original charge. The value of patience in this situation cannot be overstated. Patience might mean a disciplined choice not to act or react even though everything in your body is screaming, terrified for your adult-child. Patience may mean the choice to allow a specific amount of time to pass before you form or express any opinion about your adult-child's situation — time you may feel is "dangerous" to waste for fear of your child becoming more deeply immersed in her new life experience. It may mean literally biting your tongue, being willing to tolerate very painful and uneasy emotions instead of expressing them to your adult-child. Your willingness to step back and allow the bigger picture to be revealed to you will result in an approach to your son or daughter that is based on clarity, equanimity and understanding.

Step #4 — Don't Argue, Coerce, or Attempt to Persuade Your Adult-Child

A mother who does peer-counseling with other parents shared this account:

> "A woman called me because her daughter was in an off-beat type of group, and their relationship was deteriorating quickly. Every time she would call home, her mother would say to her, 'That sounds like a cult to me. Are you sure you're not being controlled?'
>
> She said all the things a parent wants to say, but that are guaranteed to put up barriers between

parents and children. I explained to her the problem of arguing. She said she couldn't help herself. I told her that she'd have to or she was going to lose her daughter. I told her that every time she was about to argue or criticize that she should bite her tongue and think of me . . . She called me back three weeks later and couldn't thank me enough."

When your son or daughter presents you with his or her decision to live an alternative lifestyle, make every effort to refrain from arguing, persuading, or otherwise trying to convince him to change his mind about his choice. Arguing about this topic (or any other!) simply doesn't work. Everybody has experienced the futility of arguing, yet it is a difficult habit for many to break. The "best case" scenario of an argument is that one person gets to feel that he is right — that he has won the match, proved his point — and the other is wrong. Obviously, even when a person wins an argument, neither real communication nor real relationship has occurred. More likely, both parties are left with feelings of defensiveness and resentment. Each individual simply closes off, puts up the walls, and prepares to defend the fort.

In the beginning stages, an adult-child's communication with his parents about his lifestyle choice is often characterized by heated conversations and arguments. In spite of the adult-child's zealousness or lack of sensitivity when speaking with his parents, if a parent immediately begins to argue, threaten or criticize, this will almost always alienate the adult-child. If an adult-child knows that whenever he tries to speak with his mom or dad he is going to be met with such negativity, he naturally wants to avoid this whenever possible. The adult-child simply decreases the frequency of his conversations and visits with his parents. When this occurs, parents often complain, and mistakenly attribute this withdrawal of contact to some restrictions imposed by the new community.

"My mother called me out to the front porch of my grandfather's old Victorian house. As soon as I heard the tone in her voice, I began to fill with dread and my heart began to sink. I knew that she was going to try to argue with me about the therapeutic community I was involved with in northern California. I knew that she was going to convince me that I was using poor judgement in my choices. I knew that she wanted to let off the steam that was brewing inside of her and pass it over to me. Immediately, I pleaded with her not to say what she was about to say. I knew that if she were to convey such a profound lack of trust and respect for me that it was going to push me away from her and I really didn't want that to happen. Yet once she started to talk, she wouldn't stop. It was as if she was compelled to continue. She began to tell me about the detectives she had hired to research my co-workers, the anti-cult groups she had attended, and the literature she had been reading. Again I told her that as she was speaking I was literally being pushed away from her and that if she kept going that it would destroy our relationship altogether. I didn't want the separation to happen, but I knew that the consequences of such a complete violation of my privacy would, to some degree, be irrevocable. It was a very sad situation."

In their wish for their adult-child to change his mind or come to his senses about his choice of lifestyle, parents often slip into the same tactics of coercion, persuasion and manipulation that they fear the cult or alternative group is enacting. Usually, parents don't consciously decide to engage in arguing, coercion, persuasion or manipulation when interacting with their adult-children. Instead, as a result of the stress that parents feel, tendencies they did not even know they had will sometimes come to the surface.

Coercion is another alluring trap that parents can easily fall into if they are not vigilant to its dynamics. Many choices that adult-children make *are* of concern to their parents. Yet, when the parent tries to force his or her own morals, beliefs and lifestyle choices on the adult-child, the parent is simply feeding the cycle of coercion. For example, many cults are accused of mind-control, or of "brainwashing" their members, yet parents join anti-cult groups which attempt to counter this with something referred to as "deprogramming," which is in fact nothing other than a further attempt to control the mind of the adult-child. If parents want to free their adult-children from cultic-type choices, the first step is for parents to cease from doing the very things they fear that the alternative lifestyle or cult is doing to their son or daughter. A forty-eight-year-old professor of philosophy who lived in a wide range of alternative communities before settling into a small spiritual community in the Midwest, shares her understanding of this.

> "It was an adult decision that I was making when, at age thirty, I decided to live with my former psychology professor and a group of his students. At that point, I was very strongly influenced by his vision and beliefs, but the letters, phone calls and literature my parents kept sending me about the danger of abuse and brainwashing in destructive cults simply drove me closer to the coercion that I was already accepting. It did the opposite of what they intended it to. I had to make my own decisions and, looking back, I don't see a way that anyone could have helped me to move through that more quickly. Eventually, I did leave that particular group when I realized for myself that it was no

longer the best thing for me, but I don't think that
any family or friends could have convinced me to
go in a different direction than my conviction was
taking me at that point; and I don't see, really,
how family or friends could have known for sure
if it was right or wrong . . . It wasn't even a 'bad'
choice, just something I had to go through."

Step #5 — Seek the Help of a Trusted Friend or Counselor

If you are having difficulty in accepting your adult-child's decision, if your feelings and emotions are getting in the way of your
ability to have loving and respectful interactions with him or her, or
if you simply feel the need to talk to somebody, seek the help of a
trusted friend, counselor or therapist. As will be extensively addressed in Chapter 8 — *Sources of Help*, there is no need for you to
try to deal with these issues by yourself. However, it is important
that the friend or counselor you choose to turn to is compassionate
and able to listen to you, not one who will judge you or try to tell
you what to do.

Step #6 — Start a List of Questions

During this time of initial shock, begin to consider what are the
specific questions that you have about your adult-child's lifestyle.
Instead of feeling overwhelmed by everything that you don't know,
take one thing at a time. Make a list of the practical questions you
have about his or her life. Consider what it is that you would like
to know — not only out of your concern, but also out of your curiosity. Are you interested in finding out about your adult-child's
philosophical or spiritual beliefs? Do you want to know about how
the community supports itself financially? Perhaps you simply
want to know if your adult-child can come and go as she pleases,
and that she is safe. It is not necessary, or even advisable, for you
to immediately ask your adult-child every question that comes to

mind. As will be further discussed in Chapter 4 — *Approaching Your Son or Daughter*, there are many factors to be considered when asking questions of your adult-child. Instead, these questions you draw up now can help you to pinpoint your greatest areas of concern, and therefore alleviate feelings of overwhelm and uncertainty.

Step#7 — Don't Inquire Behind His or Her Back

One of the greatest errors you can make when beginning to learn about your adult-child's lifestyle is to inquire about this behind his or her back. Although it may be helpful for you to learn more about the specific group that your adult-child belongs to, your approach should convey a sense of your own integrity and respect. The way you approach finding out about his lifestyle will not only communicate respect or lack of respect for him, but it will also have a direct influence on the quality of information that you receive. Be direct and clear with him about your wish to know whatever details of his life interest you. Ask him about his group or the setting in which he lives. If there is a leader of the group and you would like to speak with him or her, ask your adult-child if this is possible. If there is literature written by this particular group, find out if you can read it.

Include your adult-child in your process of learning about his lifestyle. Many parents make the mistake of "researching" their adult-child's alternative lifestyle without his knowledge. Perhaps a mother is afraid that her adult-child will try to hide information from her, that she will offend her son or daughter by asking about this new lifestyle, or that her adult-child will not be honest. Nonetheless, going behind someone's back is almost always hurtful to a relationship since such behavior is often taken as in insult. A covert approach is commonly experienced as a clear communication that you do not trust your adult-child to be direct and honest with you, that you are not willing to relate to him as an adult, and that you do not believe that he is willing to take responsibility for his choices.

You will learn much more by listening to your adult-child's feelings about his present situation and by viewing him as an individual than you will through popular cult literature or networks — for when you pick up a book at the library, or when you contact an organization, the information that you get will reflect the biases of that particular author or organization; whereas when you speak to your adult-child you will receive information about his direct experience. The best gauge of the overall soundness of the situation will be a first hand report. Find out what your adult-child has to say about *his* health, *his* philosophy and *his* general satisfaction with his life.

Step #8 — Realize that Your Reactions are Both Coloring and Creating Your World

Your strong reactions to your adult-child's lifestyle probably stem from your fears and your feelings of helplessness. Whereas it is natural to feel this way, these feelings will both color and create your perception about your son's or daughter's lifestyle. In a state of fear, every detail of a situation that is potentially dangerous or threatening becomes larger than life, while signs of safety and well-being may be overlooked or ignored.

Thought and emotion work closely together. When a person is conscious of how these two are connected, thought and emotion can work for her. When she is unconscious about the interplay of thought and emotion, they tend to work against her. When thoughts are full of fear, the thoughts themselves will simulate powerful emotions. Similarly, any type of strong emotion — like intense anger, pain or anxiety — will create strong thoughts that will support the reality of the emotion. In this way, an individual can be experiencing powerful emotions backed by intelligent and concise thoughts, while in actuality being caught up in a cycle of reactivity that in no way reflects the reality of the situation. Similarly, when an individual is in a mood of openness, clarity, equanimity and acceptance, the thoughts accompanying this mood will be loving, supportive and unclouded.

Try this for yourself: Consider a time in your life when you were going through a particular crisis — perhaps you lost a job, or an intimate relationship suddenly ended, or a loved one died. Such a crisis may have caused you to feel as though your life had fallen apart. Perhaps you felt like a failure — as though things never went the way you wanted them to, that you were constantly losing ground, or that those around you were constantly disappointing you. You may have felt distrustful of potential employers or mates. You may not be able to recall any aspect of your life that was good, whole and happy at that time.

Now reflect upon a time in your life that was marked by joy. Perhaps you had just fallen in love, or had a child, or gotten a fantastic job. You probably felt that you had a whole new lease on life. Maybe you woke up in the morning excited for the day; you couldn't help but notice all the wonderful things around you — the consideration with which the telephone operator gave you the number you were looking for, the innocence of the children who passed you on the street, the freshness of the rain.

Just as these previous crises or times of joy colored every aspect of your world, so now will your feelings and reactions about your adult-child's lifestyle influence your perception about his or her situation. If you are enthusiastic about her new lifestyle, when you converse with her you will notice the tone of joy in her voice and you will reflect on the rare opportunity that her lifestyle is providing for her. Similarly, if you are worried about her, every time she doesn't have money for an extensive long-distance phone call, or each time she talks about her vegetarian diet, you will interpret this as a sign of danger — the result of some authoritarian discipline or questionable dogmatism. When you understand how your perception of your adult-child's lifestyle is colored by your fears and concerns, you cease to be a victim of her choice of lifestyle.

Step #9 — Don't Be a Victim

When going through the sometimes painful cycle of adjusting to new circumstances, which your adult-child's choices are demanding of you, it is easy to feel victimized by the onslaught of feelings and reactions you may be experiencing at this time. It is important to remember that *your son's or daughter's choice to lead an alternative lifestyle is not about you, it is about him or her.* This choice is his attempt to find a way of life that expresses his need for meaning and fulfillment, not an attempt to bring unnecessary pain to your life.

Although there may be an initial period of concern, confusion and grief, you can take charge of the situation. You can say to yourself, "I know the situation looks strange and unfamiliar (I know that I fear that my adult-child is at the influence of the leaders of his community . . . or whatever), but I also recognize that I am in a state of fear and grief, and it is likely that my perspective is being distorted as a result. I know there is another way to perceive this situation — a way that does not leave me feeling victimized and hurt by my adult-child's decision."

When all of your attention if focused outwardly — on your adult-child's group, your fears and concerns for him, and your wish that he would "come around" and change his mind — you *are* going to feel overwhelmed, bogged down and helpless. The way to turn this cycle around is to point your finger at yourself, for irrespective of the "rightness" or "wrongness" of your adult-child's decision, the only way that you can take charge of the situation is by shifting your own perspective.

When you point your finger at yourself, acknowledging that it is *your* perceptions that primarily influence your happiness or unhappiness, you cease to be solely at the effect of the external situation. Immediately, there is something you can do — for yourself! You can determine that the situation which looks like a crisis is actually more like an opportunity. You can begin to look at the ways this present situation might be serving as an eye-opener . . . a wake-up call out of any feeling of stagnancy or complacency you may have been enduring in your life. You might even start to see these challenges as a series of lessons that are being offered to you, or that your adult-child's choice to live an alternative lifestyle is actually broadening your perspective both about him and about life itself. Although these circumstances may still be painful, and the relationship between you and your adult-child may continue to be difficult, you begin to see that there are benefits to this whole process as well.

Step #10 — Trust the Ongoing Process of Life

Even if you think your adult-child has made a terrible decision about her choice to live on an organic farm instead of completing her Master's degree in journalism, and even if you are convinced that she is being subtly or directly coerced into taking on ideas that are not essentially true for her, you can simply trust in her inherent intelligence, have faith that the basic goodness of life itself will guide her through this process, and hope that however it turns out, she will become wiser as a result.

Human beings are resilient — they can bounce back with enormous strength and vitality from even the most turbulent of circumstances. Consider the storms you have weathered in your own life. Think about a time when you had hit bottom — a time when you thought things couldn't get any worse. Think about who and what was most helpful to you during this period. How did you want people to act toward you at this time? What helped you to relax and what contributed further to your anxiety? Recall the period of "descent" into this situation. Was there really anybody who could have persuaded you to do anything other than what your convictions and beliefs were prompting you to do?

Keep in mind that your adult-child's decision is not necessarily such a tragedy. But tragedy or not, this experience that has arisen in her life may prove to be an invaluable source of learning, whatever those lessons may be or however difficult. Everybody goes through some periods of significant difficulty and other periods of great ease. Only in retrospect does it become clear that the most difficult and challenging periods in a person's experience are often the most significant turning points in his or her life. While you can remain available to your adult-child should she need anything, you must simply allow Life to guide her.

If you believe in God, whatever you conceive God to be, you can use this period as a time in your own life to deepen your faith in God. You can turn the situation over to your God and trust that your adult-child will be taken care of.

> Natalie's twenty-one-year-old son John had begun to hang out with friends that Natalie felt uncertain about. He would spend hours at a time away from home, often staying out extremely late, driving fast cars and listening to loud music. She would continuously call up her best friend, Joanna, and share one fear after another with her. The turning point came when one day Joanna turned to her, looked her straight in the eye and said, "Look. I learned that my child has a God and that it's not me. Whenever you start to doubt your son or doubt the situation, you are really doubting God. Just stop the racket in your mind and say to yourself, 'It is God who takes care of my child. It is God who brought him into the world and it is God who is responsible for his life, health and safety.'" It was in this way that Natalie returned to her normal, happy self. It was not that she no longer felt concern for her son, but she recognized that the circumstances were out of her hands, and in doing so began to feel a much greater ease about the situation.

While maintaining your integrity and responsibilities *to* any given situation or individual, when you cease to take the weight of both successes and failures of Life onto your own shoulders, and realize that Life has a far greater momentum of its own, you begin to relax into the circumstances as they present themselves, and to become an active participant in the process of Life.

As you work with the ten guidelines and principles set forth here, you will give yourself a bit of breathing room which may eventually lead to a more easeful relationship with your adult-child. Nonetheless, the initial period of "finding out" is still most often characterized by feelings of pain, upset, hurt and betrayal on the part of the parent. This is normal and, in fact, cannot be avoided. The only way that parents will eventually be able to move beyond their turmoil and into genuine relationship with their adult-children is by moving *through*, and not around, difficult feelings.

3.

*I*t's All About Grief

"When my twin boys left home and moved across the country to join a commune, I was devastated. I was furious, thinking that it was something about me that had made them go. What right did they have to leave me when I was left alone without a husband? I spent eighteen years working to raise them. I thought I was making a nice, comfortable life here. I had taken care of them, now it was their turn to take care of me."
— Jean, age 65

Grief is Normal

Jean was in grief. Grief is the felt experience of loss. It is normal, natural and to be expected in every circumstance of separation — particularly when an adult-child chooses to live an alternative lifestyle. Any difficult reactions and emotions you are currently experiencing as a result of your adult-child's decisions are attributable to grief. In fact, any parent who fully allows his or her child the internal and external freedom necessary for him to mature into adulthood, must go through grief.

In one way, all of life is a process of grief, for life is a constant flow of loss and gain, devastation and renewal. Although it may show up differently in each case, everybody grieves — infants, children, adults, elderly people and even animals. Something must be "lost" or let go in order for something else to be gained or something new to show up. Yet, no matter how appealing the "new" appears to be, the "old" must nonetheless be grieved. Even when a family moves into that large new house they have been dreaming of for years, they still feel a sense of loss about leaving their old neighbors. They still miss the slanted steps that wound up the stairs of the small rental house, and the dandelions that grew in the yard.

Sometimes grief comes in large doses — such as when a parent or spouse dies; sometimes it comes in minor everyday losses such having to miss your dinner engagement because you could not find a babysitter. Nonetheless, it is all grief, and there is no way to avoid it.

Life is a process of continual change, and, when seen from a wider perspective, there is a parallel process of grief that a parent must pass through from the moment of his or her child's birth. The grief that parents feel when their adult-children choose to live an alternative lifestyle is but one of the many losses in their lives.

Grief in relationship to one's children begins the moment that the pregnant mother releases her infant into the world for the first time. Despite her joy, she also feels the loss of containing that being inside of her. When her infant ceases to nurse from her breast and begins to seek food from other sources, a mother feels the loss — the first inklings of her child moving away from her. When their child first begins to attend school, although they may concurrently feel excited for him or her, parents know that their son or daughter will now be exposed to influences and channels of information other than those they can control, and they may feel uneasy about this. This letting go never stops. Parents watch with mixed emotions as their son or daughter begins a first job, goes to college or moves away from home. More and more they feel their "child" slipping away and this hurts. When the child falls in love for the first time, Mom or Dad must face the fact that there is another person who is becoming the central focus of their child's love.

There is no easy way around it. A parent must increasingly grieve the loss of influence and control over his or her adult-child's life in order to allow her to seek knowledge and experience from other sources in her environment and to become her own person. Even if a parent's relationship with his or her spouse may be deepening, even if mutual understanding is growing, even if career and personal interests are blossoming, parents will be simultaneously feeling the loss of what is being taken away.

It is not only the mother or father who feels these losses. The adult-child grieves too! A young person experiences a loss of innocence when exposed to the harshness of the world — the abuse, violence and vast gullies of separation that exists between people. As our children mature, they too are constantly faced with the loss of security — be it their privileged status as an only child, the loss of a familiar school or group of classmates, or the break-up of a treasured friendship. Parents and children both must cope with a continual loss of their illusions about life, as life continually reveals to them that it is not as they imagined it to be. Even our great times of prosperity, joy and gain are interwoven with the cycles of loss. If we deny the grief and loss that are inherent in life, we also deny the truth of a major part of our experience. Somewhere inside of ourselves we are diminished; and we lose again.

Recognizing Grief

Your grief will often show up in ways you don't expect. The term "grief" is often associated with images of intense mourning, excessive crying and consuming pain. However, grief need not include any of these things. A complete grieving process can take place without shedding a tear. Grief may contain qualities of increased perception and tenderness because when one is grieving his or her heart is open. Grief can happen amidst a full and highly functional life, or grief may devastate the individual for a time and completely disrupt the normal flow of daily activities.

Grief is not any one feeling or emotion. A whole series of interwoven threads comprised of behaviors, emotions, physical sensations and thoughts constitute the ongoing process of grief. We each grieve in our own unique way — a way that is often far different from the stereotypical picture.

If you are unfamiliar with the various ways that grief manifests, when you find yourself doing, saying and feeling things that are completely foreign to your experience and seem to you to be outrageous — such as constantly bumping into things, sleeping through your alarm, getting your words mixed up when you are speaking or driving five miles past the exit before you realize you missed your turnoff — you will begin to imagine that something is seriously wrong or that you are going crazy, instead of recognizing that you are simply in a state of grief.

Grief tends to show up in three general areas — the body, the mind and the emotions. For some people, grief is experienced in all three domains, whereas for others it may be dominant in only one or two.

When an individual is in touch with his or her body, she will know whether or not she is in a state of grief by the way her muscles feel, by her ability to digest food, by her breathing and sleeping patterns. A person who is grieving may find her shoulders are raised and pushed forward, and that her jaw is tight or that she grinds her teeth when she sleeps. She may experience either a lack of desire to eat, or in impulse to overeat irrespective of her physical hunger. Grieving people are frequently constipated — they cannot let go of their pain. The grieving person may feel manic and hyper-alert, or she may be unable to get herself out of bed in the morning to get to work. Her breath is likely to be shallow, and she may even find herself having allergic reactions to things she hasn't been allergic to since her childhood. These are just a few of the many ways that the body expresses grief.

Grief also tends to be revealed in a person's mental activity. This is a tricky manifestation of grief to identify, for the individual is usually so caught up in the specific content of his thoughts that he does not stop to consider the themes of his thinking. The parent who is grieving may experience incessant fantasies about how the leader of his daughter's new religious group is going to want to marry her, or he may be bombarded by vivid images of his son bowing down to statues, wearing white robes or praying in a language he doesn't understand. Or, a mother may find herself reviewing all the wonderful times that she shared with her daughter, and wondering if they will ever return. The parent who is grieving may find that his mind is blank and that he is uninterested in things he was previously enthusiastic about. The mind reveals grief in any number of ways, most frequently characterized by a lack of mental clarity and balance.

The grieving person often experiences her emotional life as a hurricane or a roller coaster. She might feel like a leaf in a storm — her emotions being blown from place to place due to the least movement of the wind. The slightest lack of acknowledgement on the part of her husband, or the the simplest reminder of her adult-child may trigger enormous waves of sadness or bursts of anger. She may feel a genuine sadness due to the loss of connection that characterized the previous parent-child bond, or she may feel anxiety about the lack of security in her relationship with her adult-child and the unexpected challenges that life constantly presents her with. She may feel enraged about the fact that she does not have any say about what type of lifestyle her adult-child chooses to live, or she may resent her son or daughter for causing a family upset due to his choice to live an alternative lifestyle, or for not following her advice about leaving his community. She may feel intensely angry at herself or her spouse for not being able to change the situation. Or she may rage at her child. Her anger may be directed at some faceless other — the leader of the new group, or simply some institution in general. She may express her pain with the words: "Why does this have to happen to me," or "It's not fair," and despite their appearance, all of these are normal expressions of grief.

The grieving parent may continually feel as though she is going crazy, or at the very least that she "woke up on the wrong side of the bed." Everything that happens throughout the day may be exceptionally upsetting, disturbing, or annoying to her. She may feel grumpy, frustrated and agitated, interspersed with an unexpected feeling of elation. Or, perhaps she finds herself feeling weepy and upset by even the simplest matters in life such as spilling a glass of water, or a traffic light that won't turn green. This can be an indication to her that she is in a state of grief, that her emotions are the ruling factor of her day, that she is likely to be over-sensitive and highly reactive to others, and that it is not a good time to make major decisions or to engage important matters in relationship to her adult-child.

All of these emotional responses are indications that a person is in the grieving process. Yet, there is a deeper feeling that often underlies all of these manifestations, a feeling that comes from our core. This core feeling may be experienced as a piercing wound in the heart; a raw, stripped feeling in the body; or a vast emptiness in the mind. It is the existential pain of the truth of the situation . . . the pain of the separation between parent and child. Any significant loss connects the griever with the harsh reality that all of life is essentially out of the individual's control, and that death will ultimately separate him from everyone and everything he loves. This pain is simple, clear and startlingly real. When one is feeling this pain, it is so primal and basic that it tends to overshadow any of the other individual sensations, thoughts and emotions that are commonly symptoms of grief.

Again and again it must be remembered that although the grieving process may be painful, this does not mean that it is in any way bad. Neither the parent nor the adult-child has done anything *wrong* for which her grief is the punishment or consequence. Grief is an organic aspect of life, and the pain that the parent feels is simply one of the many seasons that she moves through in the course of her life. If a parent cannot accept that this pain is normal, she will feel cheated by life and resent both herself and her adult-child. If she can bring herself to embrace the sometimes painful aspects of life, she will relax into her experience, however it presents itself. In doing so, she will learn and grow a great deal from it. The parent who is willing to go through whatever grief she must feel creates space for the true life — the life of real relationship.

What You Grieve

Although the experience of grief is common to all human beings, the specific circumstances that provoke grief are unique to each individual. A parent's loss may be so great that it feels like mourning someone who's not dead . . . as one mother expressed when her son moved to Mexico to pursue social work; or it may be a much smaller adjustment such as a mother getting used to the fact that her Buddhist son now has a shaved head, and she feels awkward when trying to explain this to her friends. Although each individual's grief process is unique, there do tend to be common themes for those parents who have an adult-child who has chosen to live an alternative lifestyle.

Oftentimes, a parent must grieve for the loss of "the child." Of course she has not literally lost him, but he is no longer a child, and her role as mother is no longer what it was. This type of grief is shared not only among parents whose adult-children have chosen to live an alternative lifestyle, but among all parents whose children have grown up, left home and begun to make adult decisions that are independent of their parents. This is what is popularly referred to as the "empty nest syndrome." Whether the adult-child is twenty years old or forty years old, the first time he or she makes a choice that radically departs from the cultural and familial values in which he was raised, his parents will react. His decision may shock his parents, for no matter how much lip service they give to wanting their child to grow up to become an independent adult, internally they are often unprepared for the reality of this.

Among mothers who have lived as homemakers and devoted themselves wholly to the upbringing of their child, the shock of their child's independence may be particularly painful. An empty place throbs inside of her when her adult-child begins to lead an independent life. Having given herself so completely to her child, and identified so closely with him, she may no longer know who she is apart from him. She is not to blame for this. Nor is her fear that she is, in fact, "nobody apart from him" true. But, until she grieves her loss she will not be able to release him, nor claim who she now is.

> "I'll never forget the day I showed my mother the map of the 10,000 mile peace pilgrimage I was planning on taking from Panama City to Washington D.C. Her face went pale, and her first reaction was, 'How could you do this to me?!'
>
> 'To her?' I thought, with a feeling of sunken betrayal. 'Doesn't she care about what I want in my life?'
>
> In retrospect it is obvious to me how upsetting this must have been to her. If my intention was in part to jar her, it was only because, after years of engaging in many forms of alternative spirituality and living situations, I wanted her to understand that I was not going to become the person that she wanted me to be. I wanted her to finally get that she had lost the one that she was attached to, and that a strong relationship between us was going to have to be based on something new."

Many parents share in common the grief they feel with a son or daughter's decision to disengage from religious practice altogether, or engage in a spiritual or religious practice that is different from the one he or she was raised in. This is particularly common among parents who believe that failure to practice according to their religion means that their son or daughter will not be saved, or will be sent to hell. In some cases the inability to let go of these beliefs results in the parent's choice to completely alienate or disown the adult-child.

When Robert joined a Ba'hai community, his mother became extremely anxious. She was a staunch Catholic, and felt that she would be held accountable in God's eyes for the "sins" of her son. She saw her son's choice as evidence that she had failed to teach him right from wrong, and feared the consequences of this.

However, many parents who examine this issue closely discover that this lurking fear is a cover for another issue. The real grief is often due to the parent feeling betrayed by the adult-child's choice — as though the choice to embrace a different religion, or no religion at all, is somehow a rejection of, or a failure to respect the parent and the way the parent raised him or her as a child.

A further reason that the parent may feel grief about her adult-child's choice to pursue a different form of spiritual life than her own is when the parent feels strongly about the maintenance of her religious tradition. She may feel a genuine loss at having raised a child who will not carry on the tradition in the way that she had hoped he would. As is the case with all grief, there are valid and real reasons for these feelings. The parent is not wrong to be disappointed, nor is her adult-child wrong for his choices. Nevertheless, these losses must be grieved. This is simply the way that life is.

As a parent, you might look at your adult-child's lifestyle choice and feel frustration about your inability to convince him of what feels so obvious to you. However, if you are really willing to be honest with yourself and your own feelings, you may discover that underneath all of this frustration is sadness and grief about the fact that you had expectations that are not being met. Your adult-child has made a life choice that is so far from anything that you know or understand, or that you wanted for him. You may feel that his decision is taking him into a way of life that makes no sense to you given the possibilities available to him. It may feel to you as though he is taking great and unnecessary risks in engaging something that is unknown and devoid of security. It may seem to you that he has made a decision that will lead him away from what you perceive to be his highest potential. It is *normal* that you would feel this way. Grief will follow the loss of our dreams, our expectations, our plans.

When Grief is Denied

For the majority of us, the need to grieve has been denied and covered by the cultural precedent of, "Be strong, don't cry, and don't show your feelings." Particularly for men, but also for women, people in contemporary Western culture are not encouraged to cry, not to let down their guard, not to be vulnerable. We are so busy doing forty and fifty-hour per week jobs, commuting to and from these jobs, filling our minds with television and movies, eating at any one of a myriad of restaurants that are open twenty-four hours a day and going to the gym to workout in between, that many of us have removed any opportunity to actually *feel* what we are experiencing. The pace of life in contemporary culture has become so fast and so consuming that people often feel that they cannot stop or else they will get run over. This directly supports the tendency for the culture-at-large to deny its grief; for who has time to feel?

We human beings will go to surprisingly great lengths in order to deny our grief. Often we deny because we imagine the pain of grieving will be much greater than it is. Unconsciously, we may believe that if we were to feel the pain of our loss, it would be overwhelming and would literally destroy us. We might think that if we open up our pain that we will be unlatching floodgates that pour forth unending tears. To the degree that we fear the pain that is so naturally a part of life experience, we will take every precaution to see to it that the floodgates remain locked and secure.

Unfortunately, there are consequences for this denial. When the members of a family finally cross paths at 8 p.m. over a carry-out dinner and they really have nothing to say to one another, or when a couple who have been together for fifteen years recognizes that there is no love left in their relationship, chances are they have all been denying the feelings of pain and loss in their lives together, and in doing so have lost the "juice" of their mutual love. This widespread emotional denial is evident in the massive amounts of medication that are used to remedy forms of illness that were rarely heard of one hundred years ago.

When a son or daughter chooses to live an alternative life-style, the parents may try to sweep their feelings of loss "under the carpet," in an attempt to ward off their own grief, and to sustain a strong relationship with their adult-child. And, for awhile, it may appear that they have adequately dealt with their feelings about the present situation. They may have discussed the problem at length and may even appear to others to be open to their adult-child. However, whenever feelings are swept under the carpet, there will always remain some residue — qualities of tension, shallowness and superficiality that pervade the relationship, leaving everyone dissatisfied. In the case of parents who have been willing to fully grieve their losses, however, there will be qualities of softness, vulnerability and realness in their relationship with their son or daughter. Parents who feel a need to paint a picture of perfect peace and understanding in relationship to their adult-child are probably in denial. Parents who are willing to feel and grieve their losses are courageous enough to allow for the natural ebbs and flows in the cycle of any relationship.

Why Should I Grieve?

Grieving is not done for its own sake, although a great deal of knowledge and even wisdom are often acquired by going through it. Instead, a parent enters this process in order to come into fuller contact with the truth of his or her own experience — of sadness, fear, separation, guilt . . . and love. When we grieve we come out of it with a greater capacity to engage in real relationship both with ourselves and with our adult-child.

"Your pain is the breaking of the shell that encloses your understanding," writes poet Kahlil Gibran. Grieving is often necessary for a parent to come into true relationship with his or her adult-child. The heart does not operate selectively — it does not remain open to joy, intimacy and love, while screening out grief, anger and pain. If a parent's heart is in any way closed to his or her adult-child as the result of any painful aspect of their shared past, a willingness to grieve can be used as a wedge to crack open the door to the heart. If a parent cannot grieve, she can still have a moderately fulfilling connection with her adult-child and have frequent contact with him, but in order to have a *truly* satisfying and intimate relationship with him, it is necessary for the parent's heart to be open. When the heart is blocked by anger and resentment, the flow of relationship between parent and adult-child is broken.

Until they have been able to grieve their losses, parents will often blame themselves and feel guilty for their adult-child's decision to lead an alternative lifestyle. A father may think, "If only I hadn't let my daughter hang out with those strange friends in high school . . . If only I had insisted that she attend Sunday school . . ." The implication is that if he had done something differently, his adult-child would not have made this "terrible" choice. First, this assumption implies that what the adult-child is doing is *wrong* and that somebody should be blamed for it; and secondly, that it is the parent's fault that the adult-child has made the choice that she has. If the issue of the adult-child's choice of lifestyle remains at the level of right or wrong — implying that either the parent or the adult-child is to blame for this and is therefore guilty because of this — grief will not be felt, and the underlying issues will not be resolved.

When these assumptions of right and wrong are not examined, a parent is likely to feel guilty and form inaccurate conclusions about the situation, instead of remembering that it is the adult-child who, due to a variety of influences (only one of which is the parent), has chosen this alternative lifestyle. Despite our failings, most of us have raised our kids to the best of our capacity. After a point, we are no longer responsible for the decisions that they make. Our guilt functions, in part, to ward off our underlying feelings of grief. As long as we are stuck in feelings of self-blame and guilt, wondering what we have done wrong, we are not able to feel the sadness beneath this. Only by feeling our sadness and telling the truth about it will we heal it.

A third important reason to grieve is to come to peace with our expectations for our children — what we had hoped for, how deeply we had invested ourselves in these expectations and what it now feels like for these expectations not to be met. The grieving process is often initiated when we finally realize that we cannot change the present circumstances, and that to do so would be an attempt to mold our adult-children into something they are not. At this point, we may recognize that the only hope for lasting peace of mind comes from how we choose to relate to the given situation. Initially, it is important for us to simply recognize and acknowledge the fact of our disappointment. But, neither we nor our adult-children will be released until the loss is felt for what it is and until we have opened to the grief that blocks our hearts.

A therapist and mother of a gay son shares her perspective:

> "For a parent to really be able to have inner space for his child's choice, to let him be as he is without trying to get him to change in any way, there often has to be a period of grieving — just grieving the loss of the fact that his child has not grown up to be that which the parent wanted him to be — whether it is that his child is not choosing to live in the same town as his parents, that he has married someone outside of the parent's religion or that he is involved in a homosexual

relationship. There are many choices children make as they grow up that a parent can control, up to age eighteen or so, after which the parent no longer has control. There are many, many choices children make that parents wish they wouldn't, and living an alternative lifestyle is only one. It is important that parents can realize this and allow it to give them some perspective so they do not continue to believe that it is their adult-child's alternative lifestyle that is the source of the grief. No matter what his child decides to do, a parent will come up against the fact that his child has become an adult and is making choices different from those that the parent would make."

The Adult-Child Also Grieves

"It was very intense. I was breaking into a sweat very often and would leave my parents' house shaking. In fact, one time after I left dinner with them, I 'totalled' my car — completely smashed it up. I had to call my parents, and they picked me up. I crashed the car because I was in such emotional catharsis over wrestling with just how to be with my folks about what was true for me in my life. It was excruciatingly difficult."

Whether it is seen or unseen, expressed or unexpressed, the adult-child also grieves his losses. Thus far, the grieving process has been presented from the perspective of the parents because, essentially, they can only attend to their own grief. However, in remembering that their son or daughter also grieves, parents can recognize that this process is a shared experience, and in this way realize they are not alone.

The adult-child's grief is not unlike that of the parent. The adult-child grieves the fact that she is unable to meet her parent's expectations of her while maintaining her own integrity. Though she may feel empowered by the capacity to make her own life choices, the adult-child grieves the loss of a certain protection and security that she was able to feel when she could depend on her parent to take care of her basic needs. She can no longer afford to relate to her parents as if she were still a child, and each time she refrains from doing so, she feels a sense of loss. Much in the way that parents grieve the unfulfilled dreams and wishes for their adult-child, the adult-child also grieves the loss of her ideals and hopes about who her parents are and about how they would respond to her emergence into adulthood. The adult-child, like her parents, grieves the loss of old and comfortable ways of relating, though she knows that this must be released in order for something new to flower in its place.

> "Although I have a loving relationship with my parents and I see them frequently, there is always a twinge of sadness that they will never know who I really am. Who they love is their idea about me. They take the few things I say and fit them into their idea of a child who has a good job, is well liked and hard-working. Sure all of those things are true about me, but I can't really share my self."

It Won't Last Forever

> "After awhile you get tired of crying. I believe firmly in the old adage, 'If you can't change things, accept them.' It took me a long, long time, but the tears cried themselves out and I went on with my life."

One of the characteristics of grief is that while a person is grieving, *it feels as though it will last forever.* This feeling is normal but it does not reflect the reality of the situation. Perhaps as an adolescent or young adult you lost your relationship with "the love of your life." At the time, you probably felt as though there would never be anyone else to take his or her place. However, because life is an organic process, forever changing, and because there is a cycle to all our feelings and emotions, you undoubtedly healed and moved on. The same is true today. In due time, your grief will pass. It is important, however, not to try to rush the process. Grief cannot be rushed. Attempting to hurry through grief is bound to result instead in the suppression of it, causing it to fester in the body and mind.

Grief must simply be felt, again and again, at the pace in which the individual is willing and able to feel it. When grief has completed its cycle, the pain *will* lessen, even if it never goes away completely. Life will move on.

The Healing Power of Grief

Grief heals. An adult-child's choice to lead an alternative lifestyle often leaves parents with a wound that can only be healed through a willingness to grieve. A physical wound begins to heal when it is exposed, carefully cleansed, tended to with love and nurturance, and given time to mend. Similarly, when an emotional wound is exposed, cleansed through the tears of grief, tended to with wisdom and care and given the necessary time and patience, it too begins to heal. Modern civilization, however, is a "band-aid" culture in which there are infinite possibilities to cover up or altogether hide the feeling of pain or woundedness. A person can watch television, eat endless quantities of rich food and sweets, or become a "workaholic," not to mention the rampant availability and use of alcohol and anti-depressants. All of these distractions are designed to seduce the individual away from his worries and pain. Unfortunately, the relief that they provide is temporary.

They do serve as a band-aid — but one that hides the grief without healing it. A hidden wound does not heal.

The exposure of grief can be painful, but an unexpected joy is often simultaneously experienced. The joy comes from touching or tasting something that is *true* and *real*, for the pain that emerges when a person allows his wound to be exposed is a pain that has always been there anyway. Though it was well-hidden, it has been lurking underneath the surface all along. When the pain is revealed, there is a certain relief that comes from finally acknowledging what is true and real. Something inside the person knows that he has lived as a prisoner to this pain, and that in order to be free he must first admit that he *is* in prison.

When the wound of our grief is open, i.e., expressed or shared, we cease to hide our pain from ourselves and from others in the same way that we did previously. We are amazed, at times, to learn that in this exposure we haven't been devastated. We can still step outside of the feelings when the situation calls for it. But we also see that the quality of life that emerges when we are willing to acknowledge our wound has a depth and aliveness to it that was unavailable to us while our wound remained hidden. When we are willing to expose ourselves to our pain, we also expose ourselves to healing.

The mind and heart, as well as the entire physical body, contain within them all the elements they need to naturally heal themselves. If we make a conscious choice to expose our wound and feel the accompanying pain, we needn't *do* anything further in order to heal it. When grief is felt, healing naturally results.

Getting In Touch With Your Grief

"The soul flower finds its nourishment in the roots
that go deepest into the dark, rich mud."
—Marion Woodman

It is not easy to allow yourself to grieve. Culture, society and all of your own defenses are jointly working together to discourage you from facing your feelings of fear and loss. Therefore, it is important to remember that you must be as patient as possible with yourself during the grieving process. Grief can be likened to a newborn child — it is raw, vulnerable and exposed. It needs to be met with caring, gentleness and compassion.

There are numerous ways you can use to begin to get in touch with your grief. First and foremost, you can set aside uninterrupted time to be with yourself with the intention of feeling your grief. Depending on your present circumstances, you might choose an hour a day, or an hour a week. During this time, you may choose to do one of several things that will help you to relax and connect with yourself.

For some people, taking a hot bath or getting a professional therapeutic massage helps them to let down their guard and get a sense of what is going on for them beneath the surface. For others, involving the body in a nurturing form of physical exercise, such as walking or dancing, helps to release the tension they are feeling and to "move" the grief that may be locked up in the body. Avoid rigorous, obsessive exercising, as this may serve to simply mask the grief further at this time.

Being outside in nature — by the ocean, in the mountains or the forest, or simply in the nearby park — is another means by which people are able to access the bigger picture of their life and the greater harmony that is always existing. Nature can be soothing and relaxing to the mind, and this relaxation may allow the necessary mood for your feelings to surface.

Journal writing is a particularly effective tool that aids in clarifying your thoughts and feelings. Allow yourself to write freely about the situation, without judging or censoring your words. If you do not know where to begin your writing, try asking open-ended questions of yourself and responding to them in writing. One example of such writing exercise might be:

*In regard to my adult-child's choice to live an alternative lifestyle, I am angry about . . .

*In regard to his/her decision, I am sad about . . .

*In regard to his/her lifestyle choice, I am afraid that . . .

You might want to interview yourself about what it is like to be a parent who has an adult-child who has chosen to live an alternative lifestyle, or write a short essay about what this situation is like for a parent.

A further way of getting in touch with your grief is by telling your story. When you speak your situation aloud to a trusted friend in a way that is not complaining, but instead expressing your experience and feelings about what is going on for you, it is possible to access a greater sense of clarity and understanding than you are able to when it is bottled up inside of you.

When attempting to connect to your grief, it is important that you be as honest as possible with yourself, and that you refrain from judging whatever arises — anger feelings, desires for revenge, a sense of meaninglessness. There is no right way to grieve — whatever you are feeling is absolutely fine and usually normal. You don't have to act on what you feel . . . just observe it. What matters is simply that you make the space to feel what is really going on . . . to get in touch with what lies beneath the thoughts and emotions that block you from your heart. The point is simply to *feel* — not to express or to think.

You may discover that, even when you allow yourself this time, you are still unable to access your grief. If this is the case, you may want to enlist the help of a friend who is willing to be there with you and help provide you with the safety and compassion that is necessary in order to allow your grief to emerge. It is also important that you and your friend make an agreement ahead of time that the purpose of this engagement is to allow *you* to feel, and is distinct from the way in which you and he/she ordinarily relate to one another. In clarifying the intention of what it is you hope to create in this time, there is a greater likelihood that you will feel safe enough to grieve. A therapeutic counselor may also prove invaluable to you in this process.

Grief is the Passageway Into Love

Grief yields way to acceptance, and acceptance to love. The grief that at one time seemed to be endless starts to dissipate in its intensity. The parent is no longer shocked by a new set of circumstances, and, recognizing the situation for what it is, begins to embrace it accordingly.

When a parent has fully accepted her adult-child's choice of lifestyle as a result of being willing to grieve her losses, she ceases to attempt to change his mind, the situation, or even to alter her own feelings about it. Acceptance is an attitude of mind, and a feeling in the heart that does not demand life's circumstances be a certain way in order for a parent to be content. It is a recognition on the part of the parent of the completeness of both her adult-child and his situation exactly the way it is. Acceptance can include the parent's recognition of the fact that she does not agree with her adult-child's choice, that this is not what she would have wished for him, and even that she continues to feel anxiety and pain about the situation. Acceptance can include all of these things precisely because, having grieved her losses, the parent has come to a place of reconciliation within herself that is not dependent upon any external circumstance.

She will find that the often disconcerting manifestations of grief will eventually give way to true feeling. True feeling comes from deep within a person and is often experienced as subtle, profound and deeply connected to her capacity to perceive the reality of her situation with clarity and objectivity.

When the parent is no longer fighting or resisting the situation before her, her heart opens naturally to her adult-child. It is as if the tears of her loss have cried themselves out, and have left her with a tender, but open heart — for underneath the layers of grief lies always an open heart.

In the open heart is a feeling of expansiveness large enough to contain all that a parent is encountering. The open heart does not discriminate between good feelings and bad feelings, or right choices and wrong choices. It is the heart of acceptance. The open heart contains a quality of depth within it that allows the individual to experience a richness and fullness in her life. It is not that she feels blissful or happy all of the time, for these conditions are also temporary, but rather there is a vulnerability and receptivity to all of life that allows there to be an underlying presence of love no matter what her circumstances are.

The open heart does not want to be protected from grief — for if it is closed to its pain, it is also closed to its love, which is its greatest gift. When people are willing to go through the grief which encloses their hearts, they come out softer and more willing to be with people as they are. Those questions and concerns that previously plagued them no longer seem as imminent, problematical and disturbing as they once did. The open heart in turn opens the mind in such a way that the individual is naturally able to perceive the situation at hand with clarity and wisdom.

Although the cycles of grief are likely to continue for some time, when you have begun to identify your grief for what it is; when you find your life beginning to once again proceed along its normal course including its inherent ups and downs; when you find yourself genuinely curious about your adult-child's present life; when you want to contact your adult-child because you miss him and want to let him know that no matter what you are going through that you still care for him — you can assume that this is a good time to approach him in order to learn more about his present lifestyle.

4.

Approaching Your Son or Daughter

"It was one of the strongest experiences I ever had with my parents. We went to a Chinese restaurant, we sat down at a small table in the corner, and I talked to them from my heart about what I was doing and they listened — truly listened. They asked a few questions, but mostly they didn't say anything. I have no idea why or what prompted them to do that, but I will be forever thankful to them for giving me that space and in doing so saying to me, 'We don't understand what you're doing, but we believe that you're doing what you really want to do and what will make you happy. Stay in touch with us and take our blessings.' It had such a profound effect on me in that it shifted the whole way I approached entering my new community. By joining the community, I felt like I was supporting what I believed in and that my parents were supporting me as an adult. I felt honored and trusted and therefore I could approach the community with really clear eyes. They expressed their concerns to me, and in turn I expressed my fears to them. We were really honest with each other. When parents will open their hearts and be honest, the child will loose his or her zealousness and just be a human being. The truth is, if a parent is really opening her heart to her adult-child, she'll get a response that is real."

—June, age 49

There is no specific formula for approaching your adult-child, sibling, grandchild or friend concerning his or her choice to lead an alternative lifestyle, and any predetermined approach is likely to be rigid and unnatural. But, as June's parents learned, there are some specific attitudes and practical tools — like active listening, showing respect and keeping the door open — that will help you to build a relationship that addresses the needs of all involved in the present situation. Remembering your desire to keep an open-mind, or to practice reflective listening, can make the difference between once again "going in circles" with your adult-child, and coming into a place of genuine understanding between the two of you.

I. ESSENTIAL SKILL: Learn to Really Listen

> "Once somebody listens, you don't have to shout anymore."
> —Alice Miller

It is so easy to assume that another person's perspective of reality is identical to your own, only to later find yourself feeling hurt or resentful when the other person says or does something that appears to completely disregard your sense of shared understanding. The purpose of intentional, careful listening is to extract a clear sense of the other's experience. Listening is a skill that is cultivated and must be practiced.

> "I've found that my relationship with my mother is strongest when I just listen to her. Often I'll ask her, 'How are you?' and then I wait for her response."

It is all too common, in a parent's intense desire to be heard and understood by his adult-child, that he forgets to really listen and instead blurts out whatever is on his mind. A mother may feel that she cannot help herself, that she is obliged to inform her son about dangerous cults or about how he will come to regret not opening up a retirement account. The results of this unconscious and careless communication are deceptive. After she says whatever it is that felt so urgent to say, there may be a certain sense of release in her feeling that, "At least I got my point heard." But, there may have been no interaction, nor genuine communication. It is more probable that the release she experiences is the result of a relaxation of the sense of urgency and anxiety that she felt, not from actually being heard.

Real listening means that, for a given amount of time, be it a moment or for a period of hours, you "empty yourself" of yourself in order to make space to hear the experience of your adult-child. You temporarily set aside your preconceived notions about his lifestyle and your desire to share your point of view with him, and instead place your complete attention on your adult-child. You listen not only to the words that he speaks, some of which might be popular catch-phrases that further provoke your concern, but to your adult-child himself — you listen to what it is that he is trying to express to you *beneath* his words. You might ask him questions in order to clarify any point that you do not understand, but you do not ask questions in order to challenge or make him wrong in any way.

> "My mother was quite reserved by nature — she rarely spoke up. I had a spiritual teacher but was living on my own in the mountains out West. On one of her visits to see me, we decided to go for a ride. Seemingly out of nowhere, she suddenly started screaming at me, 'You're never going to have a normal life. You're never going to get married and have children and a nice house. You're never going to be successful. You're never going to achieve anything!'
>
> Instead of defending myself, which would have been my normal reaction, something differ-

ent happened. I heard her — not just what she was saying, but what was underneath her words. I turned to her and said, 'Mom, I understand that you're really sad about what I've chosen to do with my life.' And I did. She quieted immediately. There was nothing left to say."

Most people were never taught to really listen. A person is taught to listen only by having been deeply listened to herself, and there are few people who have been attended to with this quality of attention. Therefore, learning to listen in this way may initially require a certain degree of effort. It may feel awkward and as though you must constantly bite your tongue or hold yourself back. You may even feel dishonest as though you are not sharing your real thoughts or feelings with your adult-child about the issue. There *will* be a time for sharing these thoughts and feelings — particularly when they are asked for — but this is distinct from the time for listening. Most people have had ample occasions to express their ideas and opinions, but few have had the opportunity to really be heard.

When an adult-child becomes aware that he is really being heard (and when an individual is being genuinely listened to it is immediately obvious to him), the content of what he says and the way in which he says it will change. It will deepen and become more real. He will begin to share of himself. His guard will drop and he will talk about those things that are really important to him. At this point, the parent's listening will be effortless; as what the parent is hearing will inevitably touch his heart.

When a parent is able to elicit a genuine exchange from her adult-child through genuine listening, she has a responsibility to honor what is shared with her. Information and feelings that are shared in this context come from the adult-child's trust in her parent. If the parent takes this information and in any way manipulates it or uses it against her, it is unlikely that the adult-child will be willing to share in that way again. Real listening, though it may sound simple, is a powerful tool in creating an honest and intimate relationship between parents and their adult-children.

Active Listening

"When we do not listen to our children, why are
we enraged when they don't listen to us?"
—*Everywoman's Book of Common Wisdom*

Active listening is a specific way of communicating that keeps the conversation from getting into advice, reactions, and arguments and focuses precisely on hearing what the other person has to say. Active listening is the process of reflecting back to the speaker — be it in her own words, or with a slight variation that expresses your understanding — what you have heard him say. Sometimes you may choose to slightly expand, i.e., extrapolate upon, what you have heard in order to understand the other more clearly.

One of the main benefits of this type of listening is that it decreases the possibility of a misunderstanding — when you reflect back to the other what *you* have heard, if it is not what he has said, he has the opportunity to restate it in a way that will allow you to understand him more accurately. Another advantage of this type of listening is that in order to be able to reflect back to the other what he has said, *you must pay attention* to him in a way that you might not otherwise be motivated to do. Furthermore, this type of listening often gives way to a deepening in the communication.

Active listening, particularly when one is first learning it, is not used in casual conversation, though later on it may become integrated into the way in which you listen to another. Instead, you engage active listening when you want to be very clear in a specific interaction or conversation. In order that both individuals have the opportunity to be heard, often each individual takes a turn at being either the speaker or the listener, and then they shift roles.

The following sample dialogue will enable you to gain a clearer understanding of the process of active listening:

Adult-child: "Look, mom. I went to live on the kibbutz in Israel because I was frustrated with the chaos and emptiness of my life in the city, and I wanted to investigate other ways of life."

Parent: "So you went to Israel because you were unhappy in your life in the city, and you wanted to see what else was out there?"

Adult-child: "Yeah. It felt like there was something missing in my life. I had all of these meaningful relationships with my friends and family, yet something wasn't there."

Parent: "You mean your relationship with us isn't meaningful?"

Adult-child: "No, that's not what I said. I said that although I have significant and meaningful relationships with my friends and family in the States, I was still missing something."

Parent: "Oh, I didn't hear you right the first time. You felt that although your relationships with both us and your friends were meaningful, you were still unfulfilled?"

Adult-child: "Exactly. Moving to the kibbutz was something I did for myself. It was so frustrating when everyone thought I was doing it to get away from them."

Parent: "So it was difficult for you when we thought that you were moving because you were too close to us and didn't want to offend us by saying so, when instead you were doing something for yourself?"

Adult-child: "Yes."

The point of active listening is not to try to repeat every word that the other has said "just right." Rather, because it is so intentional, active listening is designed to create a general mood of understanding which will minimize hurt feelings or arguments, and thus allow room for experimentation and interaction in the dialogue.

Listening Without Words

Listening is not just something we do when someone is talking to us. There is a kind of listening that happens without words. When beginning to learn to really listen to your adult-child, it is enough that you simply try to hear what she is saying to you. Eventually you develop the capacity to listen more deeply to the underlying communication that is occurring between your adult-child and yourself. The ability to give attention to another person in this way is referred to as *presence.*

With some people, although they might not say a word, you know they are understanding what you are saying. You know they are "with" you when you are talking to them or even when you are sitting together in silence. It is because they have stepped outside of themselves — outside of their own private world — and have entered yours. You feel their interest, which is often experienced as care or concern. Since they are there with you, you do not feel alone. When a person meets you with this kind of presence, it does not matter if you speak or not, or even what you speak about, for real listening is occurring.

II. ESSENTIAL SKILL: Keep An Open Mind

"I learned to make my mind wide so that there would be room enough for paradox."

— Anonymous

Like the ideal of unconditional love, keeping an open mind is a goal to aim for, not something that will come easily for many of us. Nevertheless, those parents who have had success in approaching their adult-children around the issue of an alternative lifestyle uniformly speak about the need to have an open mind. While a parent may consider herself to be open-minded, it is useful to consider just what this means as far as our adult-children are concerned.

A parent's mind is not open if he has an agenda of ideas and opinions that he is waiting to express to his adult-child at the first possible opportunity. A parent's mind is not open if, before he thoroughly understands the present situation through his adult-child's eyes, he has decided that what she is doing is not beneficial to her. A parent's mind is not open when he has the intention to change his adult-child's mind in any way, however slight. A parent's mind is not open if he believes (though this may be difficult to admit) that he knows what is best for his adult-child.

Sometimes, in their wish to be open-minded, parents convey *their* judgements in a manner that may be hidden even to themselves. For example, a parent might find herself saying to her son, "I think what you are doing is great, I'm just not so sure about that guru." Or, "I know that this wouldn't happen to you, but brainwashing is so common in alternative groups these days." Again, this is not open-mindedness, but instead a subtle form of persuasion. If your mind is open to your adult-child's lifestyle, you can afford to be straight with her, and your interactions with one another will be clear and direct.

A parent's mind is open when he is genuinely interested and curious about his adult-child's life, or is at least *trying* to be. A parent's mind is open when he looks to his adult-child for information about the *beneficial* aspects of her present situation. A parent's mind is open when he is listening for ways in which he can be of genuine use to his adult-child on *her* terms and according to *her* needs. A parent's mind is open when he believes that the capacity to know what is best for his adult-child lies within the adult-child.

This description shows how difficult it is to have a truly open mind. Some people, by virtue of the way in which their parents raised them, or the things that they were exposed to in childhood, have a natural disposition toward open-mindedness; whereas others, who may have been raised in more conservative environments, and who may not have been exposed to the luxuries of travel, or the experiences of different sub-cultures and religions, may simply not have the background to be able to understand what seem to them to be radical ideas.

Fortunately, this issue of open-mindedness is not black or white as there are many shades and degrees of it. As a parent, you begin to open your mind when you say to yourself, "There *are* other ways to be, think, feel, act and live than the way I have chosen for myself." As we discussed in the previous section, you open your mind when you are willing to closely listen to another's experience, and not immediately attempt to place it into the category of something you already know about. Furthermore, as your heart opens through the process of owning up to your grief, and as your adult-child's decision causes you to look within, you will find that your mind naturally begins to open — for when you are focused on your love, i.e., on the fact that you are still family, minor differences in ideology or lifestyle simply matter less.

III. ESSENTIAL SKILL: Practice Empathy

When a parent fully recognizes that her adult-child's *actual experience* of the alternative lifestyle situation may be sharply in contrast to the way in which she views it, the parent may begin to consider what her adult-child's experience is. In doing so, she opens herself up to empathy.

An attitude of empathy is really the key to approaching your adult-child in a way that will result in him or her feeling honored and genuinely cared for. When you empathize with your adult-child, you intentionally allow yourself to "walk around in his shoes" for awhile in order to gain a tangible sense of *his* reality. The reason you have the capacity to empathize with the mental or emotional state of another person is because whatever it is that he is feeling, it is likely that you have experienced this as well. You may not have undergone the exact same circumstances as he has, but you recognize the underlying feelings — feelings are universal.

When it comes down to it, human beings are much more alike than they are different, although it may not always seem that way. The turmoil that your adult-child feels because of his need to follow his heart, even though he knows it is in contradiction to the wishes of your heart, or the frustration he feels at not being able to communicate to you why his community means so much to him, is not unlike the frustration you yourself may have felt when you decided to pursue a career in journalism instead of going to the law school your parents so desperately wanted you to attend, or the guilt you felt when, as the son of staunch Catholic parents, you fell in love with a Jewish woman.

Each individual and given set of circumstances are unique, but the essence of human experience and emotions are similar in nature. Therefore, it is in fact not true that you and your adult-child cannot relate — you can understand one other. (However, you may in fact not *want* to understand him; you may be afraid that to do so might break your heart. In fact, such understanding may break a myriad of illusions that you have had about your adult-child or your relationship with him, or even about yourself. That's why empathy is worth the risk.)

Two Sides of the Same Coin

The following scenarios provide an illustration of the radically different perspectives by which two people may experience any given situation. The first scenario is described from the perspective of the parent; the second, from the point of view of the adult-child. These are followed by a more in-depth consideration of the emotional and psychological experiences that each may be encountering. As you read, allow yourself to step inside the worldview of each individual — that is what it means to practice empathy. There is no need to judge the accuracy or the "rightness" of each experience, just "listen."

The Dilemma of Laura and Susan: A Parent's Perspective
Laura is a homemaker and a single mother of two adult-children. At the age of twenty-eight, her youngest daughter, Susan, began to spend significant amounts of time in a non-residential Yoga center under the direction of a well-known Indian teacher. Excited by her new environment, Susan would animatedly expound the ideals of her new practice to her mother at great length. Laura was initially alarmed and overwhelmed by the seeming suddenness of her daughter's decision. It appeared to have come "out of the blue." Hundreds of questions, concerns, worries and fears began to flash through her mind. Due to the recent resurgence of media coverage about cults, and due to the sudden change in her daughter's behavior and mannerisms, Laura began to fear that her daughter's new community was perhaps a dangerous cult. Out of due respect to her child, Laura decided to try to be patient and to listen for the specifics of the situation. Meanwhile, not wanting to burden her daughter with her questions and concerns, Laura contacted the popular cult networks in order to get more information about cults. Simultaneously, Susan's phone calls became less frequent, and when they did speak, Laura noticed that her daughter sounded more and more distant.

Laura had learned that signs of a dangerous cult include marked changes in the adult-child's behavior, an overly zealous need to preach about the ideals of her group, and a decrease in the frequency of contact with parents. When Laura noted that all of these signs appeared to be true of Susan, she began to panic. She became deeply concerned for her daughter's physical, mental and emotional safety. As a parent, Laura felt a responsibility to help Susan in any way that she could. When she would speak to Susan, Laura began to ask her questions in order to find out what she was doing and how she was feeling, yet the more questions she asked, the less willing Susan was to answer. Their conversations became more tense, and the distance between them began to grow tangibly. Laura turned to a support group for parents, offered by a local cult network, in search of help. There she experienced an affinity with the other parents in the group who seemed to be struggling with similar issues. Eventually, Susan told Laura about what she had been learning about cults in case Laura had not considered these things. Upon hearing this, Laura became enraged with her mother, stopped calling her, and their relationship diminished further.

The Dilemma of Susan and Laura:
An Adult-Child's Perspective

At the age of twenty-eight, Susan discovered that there was a Yoga community, led by a well-known spiritual teacher, in her town. For several years, Susan had been feeling dissatisfied with her conventional lifestyle and her job as an office manager. Although she had become very proficient in her career, she felt a continuous nagging — as if something was missing in her life. Nonetheless, she had kept this to herself, trying to reconcile with the fact that life might not offer her a better option. When she began to spend time with the members of the Yoga community, she felt as though for the first time she was in a place in which she could pursue a life that was meaningful to her. Susan was enthused to share this excitement with her mother, and began to explain the philosophy and practices of her community in great detail, in the hope that her mother would be excited and happy for her.

As she spent more time in the community, Susan noted that the people had ways of speaking and interacting with one another different from those she was accustomed to. In order to get a full taste of this new experience, Susan began to "try on" this new language and new behaviors for herself. In the infatuation of her new life, Susan would forget to call her mother at times; she became less interested in talking about some of the things that they had previously shared in common. Susan still cared for her mother very much, but was uncertain as to how to relate to her about her new situation, as she noticed that when would she speak to Laura about the community Laura would become noticeably uncomfortable.

At a certain point, as her mother began to ask pointed questions, Susan suspected that her mother believed she was in a cult.

That's when Susan "closed down" — reluctant to respond to her mother's questions. Frequent arguments and a general feeling of dissent began to permeate their relationship. Eventually, Susan's mother confessed her involvement in local cult support groups, handed her a pile of information, and declared that she thought Susan was in a dangerous cult. Susan felt frustrated and betrayed, and began to retreat from the relationship.

Empathy Towards Yourself and Others

Since you cannot count on your adult-child practicing empathy toward your point of view (although this would be ideal), you will help your approach to him or her if you hold your own concerns gently and kindly, rather than rigidly or judgmentally.

Like Laura, in the first scenario, your initial experience is understandably one of feeling alarmed. Your adult-child's decision may appear to have arisen "out of the blue." Consequently, there may be hundreds of questions, emotions, thoughts, worries and fears swirling about in your mind — at times this may make you feel as if you are crazy; at times you may feel excited and interested; at times your fears and concerns seem so real that you are convinced that if you do not act on behalf of your adult-child immediately, she or he will suffer serious consequences.

Like most parents, you probably want to do something, but don't know what to do. You may want to say something, but don't know what to say. You might feel genuinely confused . . . at times helpless . . . at other times angry and betrayed. Throughout all of this, be empathic towards yourself. Recognize, as we discussed in the last chapter, that this whole range of reactions is normal.

In the midst of all this pain and confusion, there are probably moments of clarity. You may suddenly feel understanding, accepting and happy. Your fears may have temporarily subsided and you now feel curious about your adult-child's choice, or perhaps even a bit pleased about it. During this period, your communication with your adult-child might be effortless, easeful and mutually fulfilling.

However, if your adult-child says or does something that again provokes fear and concern, suddenly your broader perspective can cloud up quickly — all your good intentions to remember your previous understanding may leave and again you are consumed by worry, confusion, and questioning. In this way, you may cycle through the various emotional processes evoked by your adult-child's decision to lead an alternative lifestyle. No matter what, be kind and gentle to yourself. Remember that empathy is about honoring and genuinely caring for the other — even when that "other" is you. Learning to practice empathy towards yourself will be the best foundation upon which to build an attitude of empathy towards your son or daughter.

To empathize with your adult-child is to consider that she or he does not necessarily *like* the fact that her ideas and her approach to life are so disturbing to you. She may not like the fact that her decision arouses so much tension and anxiety in you, nor does she like the defensiveness and reactivity with which she finds herself approaching you. Your adult-child probably knows what you want for her and she knows that she is not complying with this — and this lack of alignment may be a source of further pain to her. The adult-child does not like the fact of your pain; she does not like to engage with you in the battle of ideals — yet she intuitively knows that if she does not follow the life that calls to her that she will be betraying herself, and that the consequences of betraying oneself are significant. She knows that in order to appease you that she would have to pretend to be someone other than who she is. Perhaps as a child she was inclined to abandon her own ideals in favor of yours in order to gain your love and approval. But as an adult she is now wholly responsible for her own life, and to place your wishes for her over her own inner direction would be to allow herself to remain in the psychological state of childhood, thereby impeding her natural process of maturation.

Try to appreciate that your adult-child may know that you think that it is *she* who is hurting you. Your adult-child probably knows that the circumstances of her choice have occasioned your pain, but she also wants to assert that the pain you are feeling belongs to you . . . she doesn't want to be responsible for your feelings. She also doesn't want to feel bad or guilty about her actions. When you do not support her in her choices, the adult-child must suffer the knowledge that you believe she has gone in the wrong direction and that, whether or not you ever express this, you are disappointed in her. The adult-child also probably feels that if you do not wholly accept her in her situation that you do not wholly accept her as a person. She does not enjoy confronting this, for it is painful; but the feeling is there nonetheless.

It may help you to empathize with your adult-child when you remember that no matter how rebellious, reactionary, kind or indifferent he appears to be acting in relationship to you, he continues to love you as his parent — for just as the love of the parent, in its true form, transcends any and all circumstances of her child's life, so the love of the adult-child for his parent persists, even if thoroughly disguised, throughout all periods of rebelliousness, dissent and anger. You are still family! Love lies beneath the superficial differences in philosophy, ideology and religion between a parent and her adult-child. The job is to bring that love to the surface. Empathy points the way.

Practically speaking, you can practice empathizing with your adult-child by asking yourself what he or she might be feeling in the present circumstance. You can ask yourself, "How does this community, or this relationship, or this life choice feel to my adult-child?" You can ask yourself, "How does my adult-child feel when I call his choice into question, or when I have a disagreement with him about his decision?" This type of questioning allows you to gain a sense of the way your adult-child feels, both about his present situation and about how he relates to you about this issue.

IV. ESSENTIAL ATTITUDE: Service

When your attitude is one of service, you cease to be concerned about what your adult-child has done to you, or how disruptive his choice to live an alternative lifestyle has been to the family. When your attitude is one of service, you are not primarily concerned about yourself; instead you are concerned with your adult-child and with the needs of the situation as a whole. You place yourself in a position of service in relationship to your adult-child when you ask yourself, "How can I best serve my son or daughter in this circumstance?"

Consider a situation that really grabbed you and took you outside of yourself. Perhaps you were the first to arrive at the scene of a severe car accident. In those moments, your attention was on the victims of the accident. You were thinking about what would be the most practical and effective thing to do. "Should I call an ambulance?" "Should I try to get the victims out of the car, or is it better not to move them?" Even if you were late for work, or had no medical skills, it didn't matter. The situation needed you, and you responded.

This same focus on the other will help you to act most effectively in the present situation. Bear in mind, however, that there is no particular set of actions or ways of interacting that constitute serving your adult-child. Instead, when you align yourself with the intention to serve, the specific actions you should take, which always vary from circumstance to circumstance, will become readily apparent to you. When you make the choice to serve your adult-child, you make the choice to give of yourself in whatever capacity you can be of use. There is nothing more important that you as a parent can do if you wish to maintain integrity in your relationship with your son or daughter.

Exploring Your Motivations

You may be saying to yourself, "Of course I want to serve. A parent always wants to give to her child no matter what the child's age." In reality, however, human beings commonly think, act and even "serve" from self-interest and self-concern rather than from genuine concern for others. The action that a parent takes may be to appease her own need to do something . . . to release the tension that is activated when she chooses not to react to her adult-child, but instead to allow some time to pass before she approaches him.

You have a personal investment in the outcome of the situation — you have an opinion and an idea about how the situation should go. It is not that you don't care for your son or daughter, but rather, to make the choice to *truly* give to him or her may mean that the needs of your adult-child will have to take precedent over your ideas and opinions.

Before you can truly serve your adult-child, you must be willing to explore the underlying motivations about the ways in which you interact with him about his lifestyle. Not that you must ruthlessly question yourself about *every* word you say to him, but you should examine what your investment is and how you are trying to turn the tides, and also to distinguish between what you want for your adult-child and what you want for yourself.

To experiment with this point, before you initiate any discussion with your adult-child or decide to take any action concerning his choice of lifestyle, ask yourself, "Who will really be served by the discussion I intend to have with him, or the action I am about to take — my adult-child or myself?" With a willingness to be genuinely honest with yourself, ask the questions, "Am I raising this point so that my adult-child might see things from another perspective and change his mind about his choice?" Or, "Am I telling him this so that I will know that I have made my point and will no longer be responsible for the outcome?" In reflecting upon these questions, you will discover whether your motivations come predominantly from a place of self-interest, or if they are intended, first and foremost, to serve your adult-child.

Recognizing self-interest may be unpleasant to acknowledge, especially at first. This new awareness might be accompanied by feelings of self-hatred, unworthiness or shame — as if this information somehow means that you are a bad person or a bad parent. Remember that you are not alone in your self-serving motivations — this is the tendency of most human beings. Furthermore, your willingness to engage in this examination is evidence of a deeper wish to look honestly at the reality of your situation for the benefit of your relationship with your adult-child. For fear of what they might discover through such self-examination, most people never make this attempt.

Giving Instead of Doing

When you are able to serve your adult-child, you will inevitably feel better about yourself and about your own approach to him or her, for you will be acting from a place of greater selflessness and integrity.

The forms of your service will vary. It may involve in-depth discussions, letters, and visits to her new community; or, it may mean you do absolutely nothing.

It is a common misconception that in order to serve one's adult-child, a parent must *do* something. Yet, it is also natural to want to do so. If your adult-child's decision has provoked a strong reaction in you, a tremendous amount of energy is released — energy that seeks to take some form of action. Instead of asking the question, "What can I *do* for my son or daughter?" try asking, "What can I *give?*"

When you ask the question, "What or how can I *give* to my son or daughter?" you invoke an inward inquiry into your own wisdom and experience. You initiate the search for a way that you can give to your adult-child from the vast well of internal resources that you possess — your patience, your generosity, your creativity, your unspoken visions and dreams. Possibilities that you had never considered previously may present themselves as the result of this type of questioning.

Giving to your adult-child may mean that for the first time in your life you don't do anything to try to help her. For the first time, you may choose to give her the space and freedom to explore for herself what it means to make an adult decision and to take responsibility for it. Giving may simply mean letting your adult-child know that you are interested and available to hear whatever she wishes to share about her lifestyle choice . . . and at the time when she wishes to share it. (The wish to *do* something may prompt you to insist that she speak to you about the details of her present lifestyle before she feels ready to.) Giving, as we are considering it here, is essentially a means of showing respect.

V. ESSENTIAL ATTITUDE: Respect the Person, Even If You Can't Respect the Choice

"One Christmas holiday, we all went out for Mexican food. I addressed each member of my family individually. I thanked each of them for their contribution to the choice I had made. I acknowledged my father's unwillingness to go along with conventional thinking when it was not aligned with his own integrity; my mother's unshakable faith in God; my eldest brother's resiliency and strong discipline; and my younger brother's willingness to take risks. Recognizing that it was the qualities that I most valued in each of them that went into my choice helped them to see that this was something that I had considered very carefully and that was very important to me."

Respect is a fundamental quality that tends to be either present or absent among individuals. Between parent and adult-child, the presence of respect is a result of the regard they have held for one another, and the way their actions towards each other have reflected this regard in the course of their lives until now.

Ideally, a child is raised in an environment that nurtures the growth of self-respect. However, due to a variety of factors including the family and culture in which one was raised, self-respect is often not the case. Fortunately, if an individual has matured into adulthood without having cultivated self-respect, it is not too late. Self-respect *can be* created in adulthood as an individual learns that she has inherent worth due to the simple fact of her existence. Whether or not she was respected while she was growing up, and whether or not she appears to have self-respect now, when parents are willing and able to show their adult-child respect, irrespective of how they feel about her decisions, they support her in developing greater self-respect.

Respect does not consist of a parent saying to his adult-child, "I respect you." It is unimportant for a parent to ever say the words. Respect is most strongly conveyed through action. Respect is an attitude, a mood, and an underlying sense of the other's worth. This inherent sense of respect for your adult-child will sustain your relationship with her throughout this otherwise difficult period. Remember, respect is always for the adult-child, not necessarily for the choices that she makes. If your respect is dependent upon her choices, it will come and go as often as she chooses to do one thing and not another.

When an individual truly respects another person, he does not lose respect for her when she orders chicken kiev and he is certain that chicken florentine is the superior choice. He does not lose respect for her because she decides to go to a small state college rather than an Ivy League university. Similarly, when a parent truly respects his adult-child, his respect does not waver when she chooses an alternative lifestyle over a more conventional one. If a parent loses respect for his adult-child as a result of this decision, genuine respect was probably never there in the first place.

The parent accepts (or at least tolerates) his adult-child's lifestyle out of his respect for her. He may not believe that she has made the best choice given her options, and he may not agree with the principles underlying her decision, but he still holds her in fundamental esteem and regard irrespective of his agreement or disagreement.

Something happens to an adult-child when her parents respect her — she learns to respect herself. From her feeling of self-respect and her awareness of being respected by her parents, the adult-child will naturally respect them and in turn extend herself to them.

When approaching your adult-child about her choice to lead an alternative lifestyle, you show your respect by your genuine interest in her life. You show your respect when you are willing to accept the fact that her values are a reflection of her integrity in the same way that your values reflect your integrity. You show her respect when you give her the freedom to make her own decisions *and* her own mistakes. You show your adult-child respect when you acknowledge the fact that she is an intelligent, independent and inherently wise individual who will quite possibly make choices that conflict with those that you would like her to make, but that this conflict has nothing to do with the regard that you feel for her. Your respect for her is evidenced in the flow of give and take in your relationship with one another — your willingness to compromise when it is called for, your willingness to speak up when necessary, and your willingness to be silent when this is what is most helpful to her.

Respect is not a given in relationships between parents and their adult-children. The *idea* that respect is present is common, but respect itself may or may not be present. Some parents will find that they honestly do not respect their adult-child, even though they may wish that they did. It is worthwhile to consider how parents can cultivate respect for their adult-child when they are aware that she does not in fact feel their support.

A parent can make *a conscious choice* to act respectful toward his adult-child. He makes a choice to speak and act *as if* he genuinely respects and supports his adult-child, even when this is not the case. He is not acting untruthfully, but rather he is calling on and enacting a deeper knowledge of his adult-child's worthiness that underlies his temporary lack of respect. A surprising outcome of choosing to act respectfully, in spite of how the parent feels, is that he or she may suddenly discover that he does indeed respect his adult-child in ways in which he was previously unaware.

VI. ESSENTIAL ATTITUDE: Keep an Open Door

Jack, a middle-age businessman and father, divorced his wife and moved across the country when his son was three years-old. Yet, through many trials and tribulations, Jack did everything possible to remain open to his son:

> "Initially, I wasn't aware of his drug use, but I assume that it started out lightly and then got worse. By the time I knew what was happening, he had already been kicked out of several schools. When I was with him, I loved him. I paid a lot of attention to his positive qualities and reflected them back to him. I never initiated a conversation with him about drugs. We talked about what he loved and we enjoyed one another's company. Eventually, his mother called me. She had reached her limit and asked if he could come live with me.
>
> We rebuilt our relationship slowly, but on firm grounds. I never wanted to turn my back on him, no matter what he did. He stayed with me for a few years, and then moved out on his own and became an artist. He comes to visit sometimes. What is most important is that he knows that I am here for him, and my hope is that this provides him with a sense of support and serves as a kind of anchor as he continues on with his experiments and explorations."

No matter the love or lack of love, the respect or lack of respect, the agreement or lack of agreement between parent and adult-child, when your adult-child chooses to live an alternative lifestyle, and you are all learning how to relate to one another around this decision, it is essential for you to keep an open door for your adult-child — *no matter what* — and for you to convey this clearly to your son or daughter.

An open door does not necessarily mean that your adult-child can come and live with you whenever he wishes. Rather, it is an attitude of mind and heart that is receptive and welcoming. It is an openness that communicates your availability to your adult-child and your willingness to understand what he is doing and what his new life means to him. Your receptivity will allow your adult-child to call on you if he needs you, and will create a sense of emotional safety in your relationship that will encourage both of you to be open and honest with one another. When you keep a door open to your adult-child, you are expressing to him that in spite of and including any differences that may exist between you, the underlying premise of your relationship with him is one of love and acceptance. An open door means that if the adult-child is ever in need — be it physical, emotional, or otherwise — and you can help him, you are available to him for this purpose.

An open door is the expression of a heart that wishes to remain open. Not that you will always *feel* open and loving toward your adult-child, or that you will be able to hear everything he says without having reactions to it. Instead, you simply leave the door open — both literally and metaphorically — whether your heart feels open or closed, as you meet the challenges that arise in your ongoing relationship with your adult-child. While it is an open heart that you ultimately aspire to, an open door is an act of love that you can make no matter what you are feeling.

> "Just as I had finished packing my van with all my belongings to drive across country to move onto the farm, my mother pulled me aside. She whispered, 'I have a code word for you. If you are ever in trouble, just say, "Grandma's apple pie" and I'll be right there.' It was sweet — the kind of thing only a mother would say. It was

her way of saying to me that she would always be there."

An open door does not have a sign on it that reads, "If you ever change your mind about your alternative lifestyle you are welcome back home." Instead, the sign should read, "No matter your choices, and no matter my opinion about them, you are always welcome."

Deciding how to consciously approach your adult-child about his choice of lifestyle marks the "end of the beginning" phase of learning to cope with your adult-child's new circumstances. In the middle phase, that of self exploration and education, this book will guide you into the process of looking within to discover new aspects about yourself and about the factors that influence the way you relate with your adult-child and his choice of lifestyle.

5.

$\mathbb{E}$specially for Siblings and Grandparents

As a sibling or grandparent, you have a unique role in relationship to your family member who has chosen to live an alternative lifestyle. By virtue of your genetic bond to him or her, you are closely linked to one another, yet the psychological or psychic bond between you and your brother, sister or granddaughter is likely to be much less entangled than that of the parent/adult-child relationship. Although you may be encountering many of the same questions, considerations and concerns as a parent would, the nature of your relationship to your family member is distinct. What you are able to both provide to him or her, as well as learn from him or her is unique. While all the material provided throughout this book should be helpful to you, the purpose of this appendix is to describe those issues and considerations that are of particular relevance.

In the interplay of all the dynamics that go on between the sibling or grandparent, the adult-child, and the parents of the adult-child there may be a tendency for any one of these individuals to consciously or unconsciously use one or more of the others as a means to gain leverage — to persuade, communicate or otherwise extract or convey information to the other. This often results in both distorted communications and hurt feelings. If you remain aware that these dynamics may be occurring, you have a better chance of staying attentive and clear in your interactions with all those involved in the situation.

Siblings

The role of a sibling who has a brother or sister who has chosen to live an alternative lifestyle is quite different than that of the parent. Although a sibling may be affected by her brother or sister's choices in a profound way, she often does not carry the same set of expectations, hopes, wishes and dreams for her sibling as her parent does. As a result, she is not subject to the same "trappings" that are inherent in the parent/adult-child relationship. Therefore, whether she happens to agree or disagree with her sibling's choice of lifestyle, she may still have the psychological freedom to express her love and support to him or her and to maintain a healthy and positive relationship. A sibling is less likely to make concrete value judgements about her brother or sister's lifestyle choice, though she will certainly have opinions about it, and because she is not as wrapped up in evaluating and judging or trying to get the other to think and believe the way that she thinks and believes, she is freer to engage in an open and accepting relationship.

"My younger brother is Native American — he's adopted. When he was seventeen he ran away — he looked after a bunch of younger runaways. They'd sleep under bridges or in empty houses. He stayed in contact with me, but not my parents — he wouldn't take anything from them. Sometimes when he and his friends needed stuff I'd bring them bread and peanut butter. It had been two years Christmas eve when he called from a town two hours away. He said to my parents, 'Merry Christmas. How are you doing?' It was obvious to me that he was making contact because he wanted to be with us but couldn't bring himself to say it. My parents wouldn't invite him; they wanted him to say it. They were hurt, but I wish they could have just given it up. I said to them, 'He's family . . . It's Christmas . . . He's my brother and your son.' They couldn't find their way to see clearly past their pain."

If you have a sibling who has chosen to live an alternative lifestyle you may experience an array of feelings concerning this. Responses tend to range from minimal or neutral reactions in some cases, to quite severe reactions in other instances. For some, a brother or sister's choice to lead an alternative lifestyle is simply not a major issue. This individual does not take her brother's or sister's choice personally, nor does he see the other's decision as a reflection on him in the same way that a parent might. Therefore, he does not feel threatened by the way his sibling's choices will affect his own reputation or self-image. It is not that he doesn't care about his brother or sister; he may have a great deal of love as he maintains a healthy respect for the other and trusts that he or she is making appropriate choices that reflect his or her own interests and passion for life. The individual's awareness of his own uniqueness in the family system and his own need to make choices that are independent of his parents allows him to respect these same qualities in his brother or sister.

On the other hand, some siblings tend to have stronger reactions to their brother's or sister's decision to live an alternative lifestyle. This may be due to a number of factors, and is neither indicative of a deep caring, nor a lack of love. A strong reaction tends to stem either from the social stigma surrounding alternative lifestyles and cults, from the emotions that are triggered when one sibling makes a choice that the other fears may threaten the bond that was created between them in childhood, or as a result of "taking on" the parent's worries and fears. If, as a sibling, you are experiencing a strong emotional response to your brother or sister's decision, be careful not to immediately react to it — neither blaming nor criticizing yourself or your sibling. Allow yourself to take time to consider the underlying source of your response, and to consciously decide how you wish to relate to him or her around this issue.

Reactions due to a general wariness or concern about alternative lifestyles, communities and cults are common. Your fears may be based on inaccurate and sensationalized information you have learned about cults and communes from the mass media. Modern society has placed all forms of alternative lifestyles — ranging from small farming collectives to large spiritual organizations — into the single category of "cults," and has stigmatized these organizations as being destructive, manipulative and dangerous. The range of ideologies and ways of living that are encompassed by the term "alternative lifestyle" is enormous, and the vast majority of these groups do not attempt to manipulate the individual, nor do they present any danger to well being. (Chapter 7: *Social Stereotypes and Cultural Conditioning*, deals extensively with this topic.)

Reactions that result from deeper emotional ties based in childhood are more complex. Many siblings become strongly bonded as children. Commonly, younger siblings will idolize older siblings and model their lives after them, while older siblings often feel possessive and protective of their younger siblings. Even well into adulthood, when each has made independent life-choices, the childhood tendencies to idealize, take as a role model or to be protective of a sibling are still likely to be active in an unconscious aspect of the relationship between them.

Perhaps the sibling you always modeled yourself after is suddenly praying in a different language, living in a community or eating a vegetarian diet, while you have chosen to work in the corporate world, own a nice house and enjoy eating meat. It may seem odd that these seemingly superficial differences could result in emotional strain between siblings, but it makes perfect sense to a young child whose constant companion and role model suddenly starts to think and act differently, and to talk about about things he or she does not understand. You may feel as if you have been betrayed by your brother or sister.

Or, it may be the case that the younger brother or sister whom you were largely responsible for raising and taking care of when you were children has made what appears to you to be a radical and potentially dangerous choice. Perhaps she wants to share with you about her new discoveries, whereas in the past you were the "pioneer" in the relationship. Or, perhaps she has always turned to you in the past when making major decisions, and now she has made a significant choice without your input. You may feel a certain protectiveness or responsibility for her that is not unlike that of a parent, as that was your role in relationship to her as a child.

> "To my sister's face, I joke with her about her life. 'Have you shaved your armpits yet?' I often kid her. In reality, I'm impressed with her courage. It takes guts to do the things she does — going off to Africa all by herself; looking into her mind so deeply."

Where any strong reactions are concerned, the same recommendation applies to a sibling as applies to a parent: *Do not try to change the other's mind about his or her choice of lifestyle.* Focusing your energy and attention on trying to get her to change is likely to be a frustrating and futile attempt resulting in hurt feelings on all sides. Your power lies in your potential to take charge of how you choose to relate to her in the present circumstance. No matter what the situation appears to be, the degree of harmony in the relationship between you and your sibling depends largely upon you.

If the emotional or ideological clashes between you and your sibling are particularly intense and are blocking your ability to maintain a respectful relationship with her, you may wish to undertake an investigation into the source of this dissonance. Reviewing the chapters earlier in the book concerning relationship, psychological issues, stereotypes and grief, are a good place to begin. You may also get invaluable support from others who have been through this before you. Counseling can also be a useful avenue to take if you wish to use this situation as an opportunity to gain a deeper understanding into yourself and your relationship to your sibling. You are likely to discover that the root of your emotional response to your sibling's choice of lifestyle is different than what you initially imagined it to be.

Pay careful attention to avoid a situation in which you unwillingly become "triangled," or used as a mediator, in the relationship between your brother or sister and your parent (although bringing in a third party with a clear, conscious intention can be very valuable). In psychological terms, "triangulation" refers to a process by which, in times of stress and tension in any given relationship, a third party is drawn into the dynamic and used as a sort of "pawn" by either one or both individuals in an attempt to communicate, manipulate or make a point to the other person with whom there is conflict. The most common example of this is when parents who are having difficulty in their relationship with one another use their child, often unconsciously, as a pawn or a weapon to get what they want from the other parent or to make a stand about a particular issue. This same principle can apply in a situation in which a parent and his adult-child are in disagreement about the adult-child's choice to live an alternative lifestyle. A parent may attempt to use the adult-child's sibling to "try to talk some sense" into the adult-child who has chosen to live an alternative lifestyle. Or, the parent and the adult-child who has chosen to live an alternative lifestyle may subtly compete to win the support of a "neutral" sibling in order to gain leverage for his or her particular stand on the present situation. There are a variety of ways, both conscious and unconscious, in which parents and adult-children use siblings, and to a lesser extent grandparents or other relatives, in an attempt to deal with family stress. A thirty-four-year-old engineer who lives in an alternative community shares his experience:

> "When my sister called me up and in a very forward manner started giving me the facts about cults and 'investigating' the details of my spiritual practice and diet, I knew my parents had gotten to her. For the two years that they had been trying to convince me that I was in a dangerous

cult, my sister had always been supportive of me living the life I pleased. I couldn't believe it. At first I was really hurt, and quite angry as well. It felt like she had suddenly turned against me. Then I realized what had happened. I had to 'call her back' in a way — remind her it was me, the same person whose value judgement she had always respected; remind her how much she had enjoyed her visit to the community and how she was so pleased about how happy and healthy I had seemed. It's hard to be pulled on in that way."

Triangulation is often done unconsciously and even unintentionally, so be aware.

As a sibling, you may feel that you have a certain grasp of your brother's or sister's situation that your parents do not have and you might experience a wish or a need to convey this to them. You may think that you are the only potential bridge to restoring a sense of harmony within your family at this time. Or, you may be the only one who is able to understand and empathize with the predicament of both your parents and your sibling. There is no steadfast rule that says you should not be involved in an attempt to maintain peace within your family. Again, the appropriate response depends entirely upon the given circumstances. The point is to be alert to the many dynamics and emotional undercurrents that are occurring at this time, and to keep your actions aligned with this awareness.

Beyond this, you can offer gifts of love, friendship and support to your sibling who has chosen to live an alternative lifestyle. The present circumstances provide a unique opportunity for your relationship to strengthen and grow. You are both adults now, and can express a form of mature support and appreciation for one another that is distinct from what you were able to show in childhood. It is not necessary for you and your brother or sister to share the same opinions, beliefs or lifestyle in order to hold one another in high esteem.

You have the chance to learn about *who* your brother or sister is, as an adult. If you feel at all interested in your brother or sister's present lifestyle, ask about it. Use the occasion to learn about something new. Appreciate his or her company, including the differences between the two of you.

Your brother or sister is still family — enjoy!

Grandparents

Grandparents will not usually feel the same degree of tension or turmoil about their grandchild's choice to lead an alternative lifestyle as parents, or even siblings might. From the beginning of her grandchild's life, a grandparent will often assume a role of nurturance and unconditional support, facilitated by the fact that she is not faced with the same daily challenges in relation to her grandchild as a parent is. This places grandparents in a unique position with their grandchild who has chosen to live an alternative lifestyle.

Whereas a sibling may take on the role of a supportive and interested peer, a grandparent can stand as a platform from which a compassionate overview of the situation can be seen. This perspective is the result of a wisdom that can only be earned from years of apprenticeship to life. Divested of much of the emotional charge that a parent often has in relation to his or her adult-child's choice, the grandparent is likely to be able to view her grandchild's situation with a greater clarity and understanding.

As a grandparent, you have seen the way in which life does not always provide the individual with what he wants, but that the lessons available in all situations, especially the difficult ones, are invaluable sources of future knowledge and wisdom. You may well know the value of making one's own decision and seeing it through to its consequences — whether or not the decision is "right" or "wrong." As a grandparent, it is likely that you have recognized the fact that every individual has his own unique course of life to pursue, and that to attempt to alter this in any way is to restrict the freedom needed to discover one's own unique place in life. You have inevitably come to see that a tremendous amount of time and energy that could be used in enjoying and caring for loved ones is instead wasted by a stubborn insistence on maintaining endless ideological and emotional struggles. From the perspective of having lived many years, you have watched these dilemmas arise and pass away, and have likely come to understand that the only thing which is of lasting value is the love that persists throughout these struggles.

As a grandparent, you have the capacity to embody and enact this perspective in relationship to your grandchild who has chosen to live an alternative lifestyle. Embodying this perspective does not mean that you must think loving thoughts of him all the time, or that you must feel an unconditional acceptance of him at every moment. Upholding this platform does not mean that you will not feel concern or have questions about your grandchild's lifestyle, or that you are unable to understand his parent's fears, for this would be unrealistic. Your wisdom does not negate your humanness — including the arising of painful or difficult emotions, or an occasional lack of compassionate behavior toward your grandchild. However, your wisdom can allow you to be at least one individual who is able to maintain a ground of compassion and acceptance as the foundation for your relationship with him, without allowing emotional "hooks" and relational dynamics to obstruct the outpouring of your love to him.

A woman who has spent several years exploring various alternative communities and lifestyles, and who now runs a small health food restaurant, speaks about her grandparents:

> "My grandparents always saw me as a wonderful grandchild who they loved no matter what I did. Whether I had a mala around my neck and was wearing orange and calling myself by an

> Indian name, or whether I was settled down in a
> nice home and counseling people . . . whether I
> had a boyfriend with a beard and long hair, or
> whether I lived with a man who was more tradi-
> tional — they were just thrilled to see me. They
> didn't really question what I was doing — I
> think they were exempt from feeling the respon-
> sibility that parents often feel, or from taking my
> choices personally. Grandparents have a certain
> freedom to just enjoy their grandchildren."

Recognize that not all grandparents are able to provide a wise perspective and compassionate understanding in relation to their grandchild's choice of lifestyle. If, as a grandparent, you see that your grandchild's decision to live an alternative lifestyle is disturbing to you in such a way that it obstructs your ability to have a loving and respectful relationship with him, you can use this as a sign that there may be underlying issues in your relationship that you wish to examine further.

Perhaps you have had an active and direct role in raising your grandchild. If this is the case, it would be quite natural for the emotional bonds and ties between you and your grandchild to resemble those of a parent and adult-child. Perhaps your grandchild's choice to live an alternative lifestyle is something that you simply don't understand, and this lack of understanding leaves you feeling anxious. Or, perhaps your son or daughter is deeply distressed by the choice of her adult-child's (your grandchild's) choice to live an alternative lifestyle, and you feel closely identified with her worries, and concerned about her struggles. In this circumstance, if you are in any way able to provide the wise perspective that is possible for a grandparent to hold, not only will you not be betraying your child or being insensitive to her struggles, but on the contrary you will literally (though invisibly) be creating the possibility for greater love and harmony not only between you and your grandchild, but between her and her parent as well.

The presence of one grandparent in a family who has chosen to have an open mind and to be in a genuinely loving and supportive relationship with a grandchild who has chosen an alternative lifestyle can make a significant impact on the entire family. Not only would you be setting an example for the whole family (and whether they admit it or not, they will notice when there is a loving relationship taking place between two individuals), but your acceptance of your grandchild will be deeply appreciated, and may in fact provide the necessary source of love that will allow him or her to remain open to the rest of the family.

A ninety-two-year-old grandmother whose granddaughter lives in an intentional farming community shares her experience:

> "When my granddaughter first went to live on the farm, I though it was pretty kooky — that's what everybody says about that kind of thing — but then I got to thinking about it, and I listened to her, and I started to change my mind. I've seen so many changes. When I was young, it was impossible for a young woman to travel or to do anything like this. She's doing everything she wants and she's so alive. It doesn't really matter what it is or if I understand it, it's just nice to watch her following her dreams."

II. The Middle — Self-Exploration and Education

The middle phase of this process is a time in which parents may begin to look within themselves in order to discover the roots of their own feelings and responses, and to educate themselves about the reality of the situation that exists beyond any personal, social or cultural biases.

6.

Psychological Issues

"Perhaps all the dragons in our lives are princesses
who are only waiting to see us act, just once,
with beauty and courage.
Perhaps everything terrible is, in its deepest sense,
something helpless that needs our love."
—Rainer Maria Rilke

"I'm probably one of the lucky ones because
I've done some of my own psychological and
spiritual work. When my children were teenagers and living with their father, I had time to go
into myself and to learn and grow. A lot of people haven't even acknowledged that they have
that side to them. Because of my own experience, I know a little bit about what's going on
for me at this time."

In addition to the many obvious issues and concerns parents
face when their adult-child chooses to live an alternative lifestyle,
an equal number of less apparent, but equally strong internal processes are evoked. Siblings, grandparents and close friends of the
individual deal with internal issues as well. While you may be
able to *do* little when your adult-child chooses to live an alternative lifestyle, in terms of increasing your understanding both of
yourself and of the actual situation, the possibilities are unlimited.
When you fully undertake a process of self-investigation, what
you learn about yourself necessarily enables you to better understand your adult-child.

The purpose of this chapter is to provide a general map of the basic psychological territory that parents most frequently encounter. This chapter presents an overview and an invitation to begin to inquire into the source of your own pain, struggle and conflicts, but it is not a substitute for counseling or the in-depth process of self-examination that may be necessary to completely undercut the roots of your struggles. Nonetheless, the insights and understanding that emerge from even a cursory examination of yourself will assist you in beginning to open up to a life that is no longer under the control or at the effect of those struggles.

Before going deeply into an exploration of the psychological issues that are raised at this time, it is useful to have an understanding of emotional reactivity.

Understanding Reactivity

*A parent, extremely upset from having received a letter from his thirty-one-year-old daughter saying that she has decided to leave her job as the vice-principal of a school in order to take up a career in leading self-help courses, calls her up immediately and begins to plead with her to change her mind. He immediately writes her long letters, sends her newspaper articles describing the failing economy, and tries to locate a psychologist for *her*.

*Alarmed by his son's choice to join an alternative Christian group, a parent rushes out to hire a detective to check-up on his son's present living condition.

*Upon learning of his adult-child's choice to live in a small, intentional spiritual community in the South, a parent begins to see the elimination of cults and alternative lifestyles as an important "cause" that she must work for, and immediately becomes involved in the local branch of an anti-cult network.

In each of these examples, the parent's response is more of an emotional reaction than a balanced choice. Reactions, in psychological terms, are often experienced as bursts of sudden emotion that may be accompanied by an intense urge to say or do something in response to feeling. Because of the strength of the reaction, people are often unable to recognize that what they are reacting to is a psychological or emotional disturbance within them-selves, and not the situation itself. In the middle of a strong reaction, the thoughts and emotions that are triggered tend to be consuming, convincing and vivid, and are experienced as though they were reality itself. When parents can identify that they are in a state of reactivity, they have the possibility of realizing, if only intellectually, that their thoughts and emotions do not represent reality itself. Thus, they can opt to not identify with the thoughts or emotions or take them seriously. People can recognize that any communications or actions that they choose to make from a reactive state are likely to be merely an expression of reactivity and not a reflection of true feeling.

Nothing can be done about reactivity except to identify it and allow it to pass. If a person can take a step outside of the reaction itself, she will see that reactions come in waves — that the strong and intense emotions that are felt as the crest of the wave peaks, are often followed by a settling as the waves fall and even out. Reactions come in cycles. They do subside. The willingness to refrain from reacting, although it may be difficult, creates the possibility for a deeper and ultimately more balanced understanding to emerge in its place.

"My mom and I had a big argument about the fact that we don't eat bread in my community. 'Who decides you don't eat bread?' she demanded to know. I told her about the diet that we follow and that it is difficult for the body to digest wheat. 'Every culture eats bread,' she insisted. The whole discussion seemed so absurd to me that I couldn't help but to laugh. Our argument clearly wasn't really about bread, but instead her reactions and fears about the restrictions in my life, or about her concern that not eating bread was an indication that we were somehow not normal — that there must be something really wrong going on in the community if we didn't do something as normal as eating bread."

Understanding the Family System

From a psychological perspective, the overall functioning of the family unit is often compared to a system in which each member takes on a different role. A family system operates much like a human body, i.e., each part has an independent function, yet is also completely dependent on the other parts. When one part of the body ruptures, breaks or otherwise ceases to function in its usual manner, one of two things tend to happen — either the system will reject that part altogether, or the system will change in order to accommodate the ailing member. For example, if an individual breaks her finger, either she will stop using her hand altogether, or she will learn to use her hand in a way that accommodates one less finger, or learn to use her other hand. In this way, the loss is minimized. Similarly, when an adult-child chooses to lead an alternative lifestyle, it is as if one part of the body has stopped functioning in its traditional role. This often results in an initial feeling of shock and betrayal on the part of the parent. At this point, one of two things is likely to happen — either the family rejects the adult-child altogether (which is usually not the case), or it adjusts, in healthy or unhealthy ways, in order to handle the new circumstances so as to minimize the disruption of the whole system.

One common type of adjustment is for the family to attempt to change the adult-child's mind, or to try to persuade him to reconsider his choice. (This is comparable to telling a broken finger to stop being broken — it is highly unlikely that it will change.) When that approach doesn't work, the family again has the choice to reject the adult-child (by a refusal to acknowledge and accept his decision or by rejecting him from the family system); or, the family may try a new strategy of adjustment . . . again, always trying to keep the system from being completely disrupted. For this reason, old, unhealthy systems are habitually kept in use long after their time simply because it is too threatening to destroy them. By the time the child has grown into adulthood, the family system is likely to be functioning in predictable and often inflexible ways.

Given the apparent need for the family system to adjust when one member decides that he no longer wishes to serve his designated function, why would a system resist this change? There are various possible reasons for this. The first is due to habit — people are simply used to predictable ways of relating to one another that are well established, as is illustrated in the following story:

> Every time Gail's thirty-year-old son John comes for a visit, he stays out late with his old friends. Every morning after he stays out late his mother says, "John, I wish you wouldn't stay out so late. I was wide awake worrying about you until you came home." John then responds, "I'm sorry mom, I don't like to make you worry, but really I'm old enough to look after myself." The next time John comes home for a visit he goes camping for the weekend. He is having a great time and at the last minute decides to spend an extra day. Since he is miles from a telephone, he is unable to call his mother. He comes home and his mother is panic-stricken, saying, "John, I wish you wouldn't have done that. I've been a nervous wreck!" John responds, "I'm sorry mom, I didn't want to make you panic. I just figured that you would trust that at my age I know how to take care of myself."

In this way, the same patterns are created again and again, the only thing that changes are the specifics of the situation. John and

Gail are stuck in a habitual pattern of relating to one another —
one they have formed over the years. It appears that it would be so
easy to break the pattern — either for John to come home on time,
or to call his mother when he knows he'll be late, or for his mother
to stop thinking of John as a child who can not take care of himself. But it isn't so easy. Consequently, these patterns often continue on indefinitely until they are "unlearned" by an act of will.

Another reason people resist change is fear. If they let go of
their present modes of relating to one another, they fear they will
be left with nothing, or with something worse than what they have
now. We spend years creating our relationships to have a certain
degree of "comfort" — even if it is comfortable anger, comfortable
anxiety or comfortable distance. If we start to act another way, our
comfort might be threatened — we might well be mocked or rejected by the other. For example: Andrea, who has always acted coy,
cute and accommodating in relationship to her husband Jerry,
might eventually recognize that her behavior is a repression of the
fullness of her femininity. Yet she might be more afraid that if she
begins to act clearer and more expressive, Jerry will be flustered
and intimidated, and abandon her because of this.

Still another reason that a family system is likely to resist
change is that when the adult-child chooses to live an alternative
lifestyle, strong feelings of betrayal (on both the part of the parent
and the adult-child) are often evoked. Due to this sense of betrayal
there is a stubbornness to change. The parent may perceive the
adult-child's choice as a betrayal of an unspoken and unconscious
agreement about how the adult-child would proceed with his life,
i.e., "I always made sure that you had the best education available,
I gave you financial support throughout college, and now you've
decided to waste it away by living in an alternative community."
It is as if the right hand of the body is saying, "I thought you were
right-handed, you've always been right-handed, how dare you start
using your left hand!" Similarly, the adult-child might perceive
the parent to be betraying a different unspoken "agreement," i.e.,
"I thought you loved me unconditionally, irrespective of my choices.

You betray me when you withdraw your love and/or approval because I don't do what you think I should do." It is as though the left hand of the body responds, "Look, I'm still a hand! I thought you just needed a hand. I like the way it feels to use my left hand better — what's wrong with that?!" From the perspective of the body, however, one hand is of no greater or lesser value than the other, and it is obvious that the struggle between the hands is an issue of subjective opinion and an unwillingness to be flexible.

The truth of the matter is that *no one* is actually being betrayed — what is actually being abandoned is the dynamic — the habitual interplay within the old system. There is resistance to a change in this dynamic because the previous one seemed to be "working well." Only when the "betrayal" is understood for what it is, do the individuals have a chance of breaking free of the emotional weight of it. Only then can they begin to allow the system to change into a more functional, genuine and appropriate one.

Payoffs

Family systems resist change for a further reason — one that is subtle and difficult to undermine. Basically, the system has been carefully (and often unconsciously) devised to achieve a very specific outcome — in psychological terms, this is referred to as a system of *payoffs*. Individuals will speak and act in particular ways that are designed to elicit certain results in terms of the other's response or behavior.

We are likely to resist change in the family system because if we do, we will cease to "profit" in the ways that we are accustomed to — even if the profit we are presently earning is less-than-desirable. For example, a parent who was abused as a child will in turn abuse her own child and receive the "payoff" of feeling powerful and in control, instead of feeling the ongoing devastation of what happened to her in her youth. Or, in the case of an adult-child choosing to live an alternative lifestyle, parents often insist on hanging onto their biases about cults, convincing themselves that their adult-child "will come around." The profit they gain is that they do not have to open their minds to a new perspective; they can continue to deny the reality of the situation and their feelings about it.

In order to understand how the dynamic of payoffs works in your own life, you can begin by asking yourself such questions as, "What is the payoff in being critical of my adult-child's choice of lifestyle?" Or, "What do I gain by seeing my adult-child's decision as reactionary and naive?" Initially, you might think, "I don't benefit at all. There are no payoffs." However, if you are genuinely interested in self-examination and self-honesty, keep asking. Eventually, you may discover some unexpected answers. You may find that being critical of his or her religious beliefs means that you do not have to consider the views of religions other than your own. Or, you may discover that seeing your adult-child's choice as reactionary and naive excuses you from seeing him or her as an adult and as an equal. You are therefore excused from the need to take his choices and ideas seriously. You may find numerous ways in which you keep the pain at bay.

Codependency

In psychological terms, codependency refers to the relational patterns that people get locked into when they remain stuck in fixed dynamics because of the payoffs they get from these dynamics. Codependency is an agreement, often unconscious and unspoken, which is precisely (though often unknowingly) calculated in order to serve a given set of desires, needs or tendencies of two individuals — tendencies that are often based on a sense of psychological lacking or neurosis. A wife may have a codependent agreement with her husband that says, "As long as you keep it under control when the neighbors and children are around, I won't tell anybody about your drinking." Or, a parent might have a codependent agreement with his adult-child that says, "If you go to medical school and become a respected doctor, you will receive my praise and support."

When one individual in the codependent relationship fails to play his given role, however, what has appeared to be agreement and understanding immediately crumbles into feelings of betrayal and resentment.

> "One time after doing a self-help workshop, I called my father and told him that I would like our relationship to grow into something more than 'daddy/little girl,' and that I had never allowed him to treat me as a woman because when I was with him I always acted small to gain his affection. He was listening as I spoke and I thought he was agreeing. Then he asked me, 'What do I need to do?' I told him that I would like him to not call me 'baby girl' anymore — that that would just feed the cycle of me being small. He was completely devastated, as if I had just slapped him in the face and said to him that he was not a good father. He wouldn't adjust — it was too much. He still calls me that."

A relationship built on genuine understanding and respect, on the contrary, is more or less condition-free. A man doesn't make the choice to try to deeply empathize with and understand his wife so that she will make him dinner every night. A person makes the choice to have a healthy, unconditional relationship out of his own love and care for the other, and out of his desire for understanding itself. A healthy, mutually respectful relationship is the reward in and of itself.

In a family systems approach, all difficulties and problems that arise among family members are seen in the context of their relationships. *All* members are responsible for either the health and harmony of the family, or for the discrepancies, tensions and breakdown in its overall functioning. From this perspective, there is no validity in a statement such as, "My adult-child's choice to live in a commune has upset the entire family." Or, "If my parents would only agree with my decision to live off my art everything would be fine." A family systems perspective recognizes that relationship always involves a dynamic give and take between people, and that an individual must both take responsibility for the role that she enacts within the system, and also be willing to allow for change in the system as a whole, when that is called for.

Understanding a Child's Wish for Approval

"I totally want to make my mom happy. When I was training in acting, she always seemed so pleased. She'd spend hours driving me to and from rehearsals, and would always come to opening night and several other performances. As I got more interested in spiritual life and less interested in acting, my mother would clip newspaper articles for me about local auditions and ask me all kinds of questions about acting . . . I want to do exactly what she wants me to do because I feel like she's given me so much and I want her to feel as though it's been put to good use. It hurts to think that what I'm doing right now makes her think otherwise. My way of showing her my appreciation is for her to be satisfied with the way my life has turned out. I keep thinking that if she could understand what I'm doing that she'd be proud of me."

Every child is hungry for his or her parents' approval. To the young child, parents are literally God — all-providing, all-knowing and all-giving. Even before conscious thought begins to form, the child learns that if she pleases her parents she will be taken care of. Thus, children grow up with a belief, although unconscious and unarticulated, that they must please their parents and gain their approval in order to survive.

Of course, the parent is *not* God, and the child will, sooner or later, suffer the loss of this illusion — due to the human errors that parents will inevitably make, and also as a result of the child's inability to consistently please Mommy and Daddy and thereby keep their constant approval.

Sometimes, due to her disappointment at her parents' failure to be God, or due to her frustration at being unable to please them, the child will become angry and disillusioned with her parents and may say or do things that appear to be directly in contrast to her wish to gain her parents' approval. This reaction to the pressure that she feels to please her parents is referred to as rebelliousness. Yet, even rebelliousness is based on her wish for her parents' regard. No matter if the adult-child does exactly as the parents wish, or if she acts in a rebellious manner, her wish for parental approval often continues well into adulthood. In many cases, the whole of an adult-child's life is subtly permeated by this wish. If the adult-child has managed to cultivate self-confidence and self-respect, she will make life choices that reflect her own aspirations irrespective of her parents' approval. But, even then, she is grateful for her parents' regard. A twenty-eight-year-old woman who lives on a Yoga Ashram in the Catskills describes her struggle:

"I guess you could say I got lucky. Although I knew my parents really wanted me to become a writer, a professor — anything but this — and that they would not understand why I was doing what I was doing, I somehow had the strength to choose to join the ashram. I tried to convince and persuade them of the rightness of my choices for a long time until I finally I realized that I could either do what they wanted me to do and get their approval, which would mean quitting the ashram and leaving all the people who had come to mean so much to me, or I could make my own choices and live with the pain of having lost their approval because I couldn't live up to their wishes for me."

It can take great courage for children to risk stepping out on their own in pursuit of their dreams, especially when it may cost them the approval they deeply long for. Supporting them, even when it hurts to do so, is an expression of your love and commitment.

Appreciating the Role of Expectations, Hopes, Wishes and Dreams

"The price a child pays for being guided into what his parents think best for him is the diminution of his wholeness. His total well-being, the reflection of all his aspects nourished or starved, is directly affected . . . They cannot add anything to his wholeness by substituting their motives for his own, or 'telling him what to do.' "

— Jean Liedloff, *The Continuum Concept*

All parents have a set of conscious or unconscious expectations, hopes, wishes and dreams for their child. All parents inherently want their child to grow up to be healthy and happy, and for some parents this is enough. However, the set of expectations, hopes, wishes and dreams that are challenged when an adult-child chooses an alternative lifestyle tend to be quite specific and result from psychological tendencies, rather than love. Among these is the tendency for the parent to see her child as a reflection and extension of herself.

There was a time when the child was a literally an extension of his mother — connected to her through the umbilical cord. However, although the child has "come through" his parent, he has emerged as a separate and unique individual with a life force that is entirely his own. While the parent has a responsibility to the child when he is under her care (she must feed, protect, support and love him), she is not and cannot be responsible for the adult that he becomes.

This may sound obvious, and in theory it is. But, practically speaking, this is often not the case. If an adult-child turns out to be wealthy, famous, successful and attractive — or whatever values his parents happen to adhere to — his parents are proud and pleased. The parents subtly experience the adult-child's successes as their own; as though the parents were responsible for them. Similarly, if the adult-child chooses to embrace a way of life that expresses values that differ from their own, the parents are likely to feel disappointed and as if they were to blame for the circumstance. For example, when the adult-child of a respected doctor decides to go to medical school, her father is pleased with her, and credits himself for her decision. Or, on the other hand, if the son of a wealthy politician decides to go to Jamaica to open up a bed-and-breakfast, his parents blame themselves for his choice. The parents' self-worth, as well as their sense of their adult-child's worth, fluctuates at the mercy of changing circumstances.

The problem with parents taking responsibility for their adult-child's choices, aside from the fact that it creates continual feelings of either pride or guilt, is that it does not take into consideration the adult-child himself! It does not take into account the endless factors, both known and unknown, that have contributed to his development as a unique individual.

If, in an attempt to gain their love and approval, the adult-child embraces his parents' expectations and dreams for him, he may well turn out to be extremely successful, attractive and wealthy (or whatever his parents wish him to become). However, the cost of this may be the suffocation of his own dreams and uniqueness. A doctor shares his story:

"I hated medical school. 'Memorize this,' 'Do it this way.' I was depressed most of the time. I dragged my feet and passively resisted and hurt inside a lot. In my fourth year I developed a sore foot that was nearly crippling me as I began my residency. It seemed to be my body's way of resisting walking, to avoid stepping into more of this stuff which didn't feel good. It cleared up when I began practicing non-traditional medicine. This script that the only way to be OK is to follow in Dad's footsteps and be a family doctor has run out. I can make my own script and be what and who I want to be."

— John W. Travis, *M.D., The Wellness Workbook*

We naturally have hopes and dreams for our adult-children. Often, we are still trying to gain the approval of *our own parents* by showing them that we can raise healthy and successful children. In addition, most of us have invested years of time, money and energy into the upbringing of our children and sincerely wish the best for them.

However, we should remember that it is impossible for our adult-children to fulfill our precise expectations. Due to the pervasiveness of unconscious expectations, however, we will often feel disappointed if our adult-children manifest even a slight variation of what we had hoped for, like being upset if our son or daughter chooses to go to law school instead of medical school. Furthermore, if our primary wish is for our adult-child to live to the fullest of his or her potential, we must not forget that because he is a unique individual with dreams of his own, he will more likely choose a lifestyle that to some degree differs from what we imagined for him.

The following questions will help you to recognize the expectations that you hold for your adult-child. You may want to write about them, to gain clarity for yourself, or use them as a point of departure in discussion with your spouse, a trusted friend or a counselor.

*What are the dreams that I have always had for my adult-child? How will I feel if he never fulfills these?

*Do I have a picture in my mind of what my adult-child's life *should* look like (i.e., marriage, grandchildren, or spending holidays together)?

*What are the expectations or wishes that I have for my adult-child that are based on making me look good to the people around me and the society I live in — be it the church group, the town, my extended family or my spouse?

*What is it that I always dreamed of, but perhaps was unable to accomplish (perhaps due to marriage, financial problems, etc.)? Is there any way in which I hope that my adult-child will fulfill this dream for me?

*Are there ways in which I show disapproval for certain choices that my adult-child makes — either directly or indirectly?

*Am I satisfied that I have done the best I could as a parent in raising my adult-child? Do I fell all right about whatever type of decisions he now makes in terms of his choice of lifestyle?

*Am I willing to sacrifice my own preferences about my adult-child's lifestyle in favor of what she wants?

In addition to the spoken or unspoken expectations that an adult-child feels from her parent, remember that she is also struggling with these expectations within herself. Her dilemma is not necessarily the result of her own doubts or insecurities about her choice of lifestyle, but is often due to her *internalization* of her parent's expectations for her.

Internalization is the process by which the adult-child literally absorbs the expectations (beliefs, attitudes, hopes, etc.) of the parent to such a degree that these attitudes are experienced by the adult-child as her own. In this way, the adult-child who chooses to live an alternative lifestyle is defying the pressure of expectations both from within as well as outside of herself.

Expectations are a heavy burden to bear. It is all-too-common for men or women to devote their entire lives to fulfilling their parents' expectations of them, regardless of whether or not these expectations have ever been stated . . regardless of whether they are close or distant from their families . . . regardless of whether the parents are still alive or not!

Sometimes, as in the story of Matthew below, the pressure of expectations is felt so intensely by the adult-child that he finds himself caving in under them, and thus reacts to this in marked ways:

> Matthew's father, a wealthy New England lawyer, had planned for his son to follow in his footsteps since the time he was a child. Matthew was raised hearing his parents brag to their friends about how brilliant he was and what a fine partner he would make in the firm. His parents were insistent on their wishes, and often made subtle comments and gestures to suggest how disappointed they would be if he didn't succeed his father in his practice. According to his parents' wishes, Matthew excelled in all of his schooling and graduated Harvard law Magna Cum Laude. Meanwhile, his father had already set up his desk at the company and was awaiting Matthew's completion of his bar exam. According to plan, Matthew passed his test. However, instead of joining the firm, he handed his father his degree and exam certificate, bought a plane ticket to Australia, and has lived there practicing as a successful photojournalist for the past twenty years.

Understanding Alienation

"One of my little cousins called me 'Vishnu' (the name I was given by my spiritual teacher). When my father heard this he started yelling at this little kid to never use that name again. I've talked to him a couple of times and told him, 'The name doesn't make any difference. I'm still your son. I'm always going to be your son; nothing can change that.' He wouldn't hear it, he wouldn't take it in, he just got all flustered. To me it hasn't changed anything — it hasn't changed the fact that he's still my father and that I'm still his son. For him, it was a huge slap in the face, to change the name he gave me — as though I wasn't his son anymore because I changed the name that he gave me. We hardly talk anymore . . . There was a lot of sadness in me about wanting things to be different — wishing he hadn't taken this thing about my name and used it against me. But he did, and I have to accept that. I have to accept that he's never going to embrace what I do — ever. Basically, he's written me off. It was a problem for me for years, but I've actually come to the point where I've released myself of the burden of taking responsibility for his pain about this."

Alienation is not a given in every case where an adult-child chooses an alternative lifestyle, but it does happen. Commonly a period of alienation occurs as both parents and adult-children learn to adjust to one another given the new circumstances of the adult-child's lifestyle. At times, it is the parent who alienates, or disowns the adult-child; at other times, the adult-child cuts off contact with his or her parents. When an individual alienates another, he or she is using this as a tool for some purpose. Some parents alienate their adult-child because of what he is doing, or because the stand that he is making is just too painful for the parent to face, such as when an Orthodox Jewish father who simply cannot handle his daughter marrying a Catholic man, rejects her because of this. At other times, the parent is so angry at his adult-child that he can't stand to be faced with the object of his anger, such as the furious mother who disowns her daughter for marrying a Black man. Still other times, alienation is used as a threat in an attempt to manipulate the other person into changing his mind or acting differently. Janet, in the story below, cut her parents off primarily to make the statement, "If this is the way you're going to treat me, you're going to lose our relationship."

> Janet couldn't deal anymore with the pressure of her parents' demands that she quit the psychotherapy she was in, and stop leading the self-help seminars. She became fed up the the guilt-provoking notes and messages they would leave her, and the continual attempts to subtly criticize her lifestyle and convince her to change her mind. Eventually, she cut off contact with them to exemplify her absolute frustration with the relationship. It was her way of saying, "This kind of relationship doesn't work for me. Until we can relate in a way that is not degrading and hurtful to one another, I can't be in contact with you." Nine months later, Janet wrote her parents a letter and reinitiated contact with them. Since that time their ways of interacting with one another have been more respectful and considerate.

For some people, a period of temporary alienation is necessary in order to be able to integrate the new circumstances of their lives. For others, alienation is created from a lack of sensitivity and compassion, and may thus go on indefinitely . . . and unnecessarily. Regardless, if you have alienated your adult-child, or have been alienated by him or her, you can question yourself about what is trying to be conveyed in this circumstance. You can ask yourself, "What is the message here?" "What am I trying to communicate by this gesture?" Or, "What is my adult-child trying to communicate to me?"

You may or may not have a choice about how long this period of alienation lasts. Frequently, it is brief; other times it is long-term. If your adult-child is refusing to speak with you, there is little you can do aside from keeping the door open on your side and making an effort to understand why it is bolted shut on the other. If you have alienated your adult-child, you can ask yourself if there isn't a clearer way that you could communicate to him or her. Whereas short-term alienation is relatively common, long-term alienation is definitely a sign that something has gone awry in the relationship.

Understanding Projection

Psychologically speaking, projection is the process by which we displace the origin of certain thoughts and emotions, placing them onto someone or something outside of ourselves. More simply, we all experience thoughts and emotions that we don't like, are uncomfortable with, and wish were not there. In order to rid ourselves of this internal discomfort, we place these feelings and ideas on someone or something outside of ourselves. We then proceed, often with great force, to resist and defend against this person or thing we have projected onto. In this way, we not only attempt to rid ourselves of these uncomfortable feelings, but by fighting against them . . . pushing them still farther away, we attempt to deny their existence.

For example, a parent who learned, as a child, that his was the only true religion and that failure to practice that religion meant condemnation to hell, may have also learned to suppress all of his curiosity about who or what God is, and about the belief systems of other religions. When his adult-child chooses to live at a Buddhist meditation center, or a Quaker farm, this parent's ancient fears are stirred. Without even remembering his own original curiosity, or without questioning the assumptions upon which his fear is based, he *projects* this fear onto his adult-child and becomes terrified for her, convinced that she will not be "saved" or that she will be sent to hell. The fear that he feels originates from his *own reality*, and does not actually take into account the actual circumstances of his adult-child's life.

Another example is the parent who, when her adult-child tells her that he has chosen to live on an organic farm, is immediately convinced that he is in a dangerous cult and that "all cults con their members into giving all of their money to their leaders." The parent projects this fear onto her adult-child and then creates a scenario that will confirm her suspicion. The parent might ask her adult-child, "Are you making a good living in your community?" The adult-child may respond, "We all work together and pool our resources, but I have everything I need." The parent then takes that response, panics that her adult-child is being conned out of his money, that he is being manipulated into giving away valuable skills for free, and that he is being forced to work excessively without pay. She concludes that this is a circumstance of "brainwashing," and makes plans to have him kidnapped and deprogrammed. What really happened in this situation is that the parent asked her adult-child if he was making a good living in his community, and the adult-child responded that the community as a whole was working together and pooling their resources. That's all, the rest was projection.

These scenarios, although more extreme than the way some parents respond (and less extreme than others!) exemplify the way that projection works. Projection can also work in subtler ways, however. For example, a parent may be aware of a certain wildness inside of himself that he has never expressed due to a fear that he would be rejected if he did. He sees his adult-child's choice to study and practice Native American spirituality as an expression of that wildness and becomes afraid that his adult-child will be rejected. The parent, in turn, projects his fear onto his adult-child and rejects her choice, thereby making his projection into a reality. Furthermore, it is likely that all of this is happening beneath the parent's conscious awareness.

What is so tricky about projections is that they are completely convincing to the person who is enacting them. The person who is projecting is likely to be unaware of the aspects of himself that he is denying. To him, his projection is *the* reality. However, when we are aware that the dynamic of projection is working, we can begin to identify it. When we feel a certain emotional charge or a vehement conviction about something, this is a good time to stop and question ourselves about what we might be projecting onto the situation that is not actually there.

The process of increasing awareness about our projections happens slowly. But, it is one more way that we can work our way through the obstacles that separate us from a relationship with our adult-child that is loving and true.

Understanding Your Own Mind

When you begin to explore your own psychology, you start to become acquainted with your mind. You might assume that you automatically know your own mind since you live with yourself all the time, but in actuality the mind has such subtle maneuvers that most people are rarely able to clearly see the full scope of its operations. When you begin to watch carefully how your mind works, it ceases to have the same power over you as it once did.

Understanding the full depth and intricacies of your mind is a labor of many years and great attention. However, every little bit helps. Here's how to begin:

Make the decision that for a few minutes a day, you will keep tabs on your thought process. As

you go about your regular daily activities, allowing your mind to work as it always does, simply
notice the kinds of thoughts you are having. You
may discover that you are having critical thoughts
— "Why did Johnny spill the milk again today at
breakfast?" "Why did Jim have to leave his
clothes on the floor?" "That damn stop-light
won't turn green." "When will my secretary finally learn I only like one cream in my coffee?"
These thoughts may or may not have validity to
them, but a step outside of the regular thought
process will enable you to recognize that you are
in a constricted state of mind in which you are
likely to be easily angered or disturbed. Similarly,
you might notice you are having kind thoughts.
"Sweet Johnny, when you're two years old you
just like to spill your milk." "My secretary really
works hard, I'm quite fortunate to have found
her." "What a lovely day it is outside." In this
way your realize that your mind is open and you
are in a generally caring mood.

When you begin to know your mind, you have
the possibility of taking or leaving the thoughts it
kicks up. This does not mean the thoughts will
cease to come, for the mind produces an endless
stream of thoughts, stories and ideas. Instead,
you can remind yourself that you are in an angry
(happy, anxious, sad) state of mind, that this type
of mind-set breeds angry, happy, anxious or sad
thoughts, and that when your mind-state changes
your thoughts and ideas about yourself and your
adult-child are likely to change. You begin to
take more control of your life!

In this chapter, we have been considering the psychological issues that arise for us as if they were *ours* alone. While it is true that there are issues that arise that are specific to an individual, there is also a culturally-based, collective psychology of which everyone is a part. It is important to recognize the way that your attitudes and beliefs are shaped by the culture in which you live, for although you must take responsibility for your psychological issues and attitudes, you need not feel guilty, as though you were the cause of them. Chapter 7 will assist you in recognizing the way in which you are influenced by your culture, and will help you to view your adult-child's lifestyle from a wider perspective.

7.

The Role of Social Stereotypes and Cultural Conditioning:
"Just Because It's Different, Doesn't Mean It's Bad"

Knowingly or unknowingly, consciously or unconsciously, social stereotypes and cultural norms comprise the foundation of our worldview — including the way we think, talk, dress, eat and act. Social stereotypes refer to a set of common assumptions shared among members of a given society concerning a specific group of individuals. Cultural conditioning refers to the way in which the individuals in a particular culture learn to embrace those attitudes, modes of perception and worldviews upheld by the people of that place and tradition. Cultural conditioning happens automatically by virtue of an individual being born into a particular culture.

The depth to which your perspective of your adult-child's, sibling's, grandchild's or friend's lifestyle is influenced by social stereotypes and cultural norms cannot be overestimated. Social stereotypes and cultural norms are an essential component of the human psyche — for they enable the individual to know how to function effectively within a very complex culture. Beyond right or wrong, the simple truth is that people are strongly influenced by these factors. Our task, first of all, is to acknowledge how pervasive social stereotypes and cultural conditioning are in our lives, and secondly, to decide if we are willing to have a detrimental influence on the way in which we perceive and relate to our adult-children.

The Fabric of Human Thought and Behavior

"One of the deepest impulses in the very social human animal is to do what he perceives is expected of him."

—Jean Liedloff, *The Continuum Concept*

Cultural and social influences comprise the very fabric of human thought and behavior, meaning, that from the moment of birth, we are immersed in a pre-existing set of social behaviors that govern every possible domain of human life. As infants, although the mind has not yet begun to conceptualize reality in terms of cohesive thoughts, we are already at the effect of the society and culture into which we are born. As we grow up, we learn to fit our reality into a set of concepts and beliefs that are appropriate to our particular culture and society. Similarly, the mannerisms which we develop — ranging from how we pick up a fork, to how we smile — are the result of years of observation and imitation of the environment in which we are raised.

What is unique to us is both the specific set of circumstances that we have been born into, such as our family, religion and socioeconomic class, as well as our *True Essence* which is continuously attempting to express itself through the learned behavior of our social and cultural conditioning.

This Essence may only reveal itself when we become aware of the ways in which we have been influenced by social and cultural norms. Not that these ways of behavior will cease to inform much of the way that we think or act, but rather, we will cease to be blindly guided by these forces. In doing so we open up the possibility for expressing what is most essentially true of us, irrespective of cultural and social influences. It is this Essence that may also reveal itself when, as parents, we become aware of the degree to which social stereotypes and cultural conditioning influence our perceptions of our adult-child. This recognition creates an atmosphere of acceptance and possibility which invites our adult-child to express himself or herself to us fully, and more essentially.

While it may be unsettling to comprehend the extent to which we are influenced by forces and factors beyond ourselves, this very understanding opens up the possibility of a life that is free of these binds. Discovering the ways in which we view our adult-children and their lifestyle choices through the lens of our social and cultural conditioning not only enables us to open up with greater clarity to the reality of *their* experience, but further provides us with the knowledge of the ways in which *our* beliefs about various aspects of life are equally impacted by these influences.

"When I came back from India I was wearing orange robes and beads around my neck with a pendant of my guru attached to it. I would practice Tai Chi, a form of martial arts, on my parents' front lawn in the suburbs. After about a week of this, my father kindly asked me if I would be willing to practice in the back yard. I was terribly offended, and highly reactive to what I considered to be a sign of disrespect for me. In retrospect, I am stunned by my insensitivity to his predicament. It wasn't about respect or lack of respect; instead, here was his daughter fresh back from the unknown land of India, dressed in orange, doing movements in slow motion on the front lawn. What would the neighbors think? My poor father! It's not that what I was doing was in any way wrong, but how could he be expected to understand?"

What Are Your Stereotypes?: An Exercise in Discovery

"My father asked me one day, 'How are things going on the hippy commune?' I said to him, 'Why do you think I live in a hippy commune (I actually live in a Hindu-based, spiritual community)?' He said, 'Well, you guys wear sandals, don't you?' 'Yes,' I responded. I got his logic. It went something like: Hippies wear sandals. People in your community wear sandals. Therefore, you all must be hippies.' "

The following exercises are intended to help you discover the specific stereotypes that you have concerning alternative lifestyles, spirituality, success, etc. These exercises encourage you to engage in stream-of-consciousness writing — a kind of spontaneous writing that is done with no prior thought or evaluation. Stream-of-consciousness writing allows information to surface that may be otherwise unavailable when the mind is busy censoring and judging the specific thoughts that arise in our consciousness. This is nothing to be concerned about — everybody has an unconscious. In bringing what is unconscious into the light of awareness, we gain the opportunity of using this information in order to form a perspective that is clear and well-informed. In doing the exercises:

1. Limit yourself to five minutes of writing per exercise. Do one exercise at a sitting, or take twenty minutes or so and do all four; one after the other. The former approach is suggested if you are having difficulty with any particular concept, whereas the latter is suggested if you would like to gain an overall sense of your stereotypes about alternative lifestyles.

2. Keep your pen moving — that is, try to write continuously even if it seems as though you are writing nonsense or keep repeating the same thing. Even if your mind "goes blank," it is important to keep the pen moving.

3. Refrain from judging or evaluating your writing as you go along; there will be ample opportunity for analysis and consideration following the exercises. Remember that these exercises are not about brilliance or great writing ability. They are simply a way to access information from within yourself. The more freedom you allow yourself with these exercises, the more value you will gain from them.

Example: Stream-of-consciousness writing exercise on the term "COW." COW: Black and white. Moo. Hay. Cows. Don't know what to write about cows. Milk. Cow milk. Goat milk. I don't like this. I feel silly. Farm. Beef. Slaughter. Cow. Mind blanking. Holstein cows. Brown cows. Yogurt. Farm. Cheese. Moo. Big eyes . . . (When five minutes are complete, cease writing).

EXERCISE #1: Stream-of-consciousness writing exercise on the term "CULT."[3]
Sit in a quiet place where you can see a clock or a watch. Have a pen or pencil and paper ready. Time yourself for five minutes. When the time begins, place your pen or pencil on the page and begin to write anything that comes to mind when you think about the word "CULT." Begin.

If "cult" or the other words suggested in these exercises do not specifically relate to your situation, there are many other terms, that are useful to explore in this manner including: GOOD CHILD/BAD CHILD, SUCCESS/FAILURE, DRUGS, GOD, COMMUNE, MORALS, RESPONSIBILITY, FREEDOM, COMMUNITY, etc. Feel free to explore any other relevant terms, especially the "trigger" words for you. The words listed above are generally associated with some alternative lifestyles that commonly evoke peoples' stereotypes; they are by no means exclusive.

EXERCISE #2: Stream-of-consciousness writing exercise on the term "ALTERNATIVE LIFESTYLE." Follow the same directions as those listed for Exercise #1 and begin writing.

EXERCISE #3: Stream-of-consciousness exercise on the term "GURU." Again, according to the directions stated in Exercise #1, begin writing.

EXERCISE #4: Stream-of-consciousness exercise on the term "SPIRITUALITY." Once again, follow those instructions listed in Exercise #1 and begin writing.

When you have completed the exercise or exercises, review what you have written. Remember, the key to extracting value from these exercises is to refrain from judging or evaluating them. In the process of reviewing your writing, the stereotypes that you associate with any given term or concept may become apparent. Not that everything you have written is indicative of a stereotype or unconscious idea pertaining to the given subject, but you may discover that it is quite revealing. When you are willing to "let down your guard" to yourself in this way, your preconceived notions and ideas will automatically surface.

Interestingly, many people who do these exercises come up with similar lists of associations. The reason is that the members of any given culture will share in common many of their stereotypes, belief systems and worldviews. It is easy to think, "But I don't view *my* adult-child like that." However, even if you do not consciously consider yourself to have stereotypical ideas about any of the terms listed above, and even if you rarely speak or act from the basis of these stereotypes, there are still a set of ingrained beliefs that result from being raised in any particular culture that few, if any, members of that culture are exempt from.

Moving Past Our Stereotypes

How do we come to see our sons and daughters for who they are outside of the confines of our social stereotypes and cultural conditioning? Most importantly, we remember that no matter what choices our adult-children have made, they are still family!

> Maria's daughter Pamela was a "normal" kid in her youth — smart, social and active in school activities. Beyond this, Maria respected her a great deal for her zest for life and her sense of adventure. However, beginning in high school, she was traveling to Third World countries to do social work, and campaigning for Greenpeace. In college, Maria watched her go through a tie-dye, torn jeans, 'hippy phase,' into political activism where she was protesting everything under the sun, and then sample numerous spiritual practices ranging from Hasidic Judaism to shamanism. Everything that carried a social stigma or stereotype attached to it, Pamela did. Maria had to continually struggle between the strong social biases about her daughter's activities, and her deeper trust in, and respect for, Pamela's quest for understanding and desire to help others.

When you are able to refrain from judging and evaluating both yourself and your adult-child, you may then start to take an inventory of the social stereotypes that are influencing your present perception. You can begin by asking yourself questions such as: "Is it helpful both to myself and to my adult-child to view the present situation in this way?" "Where did my ideas about my adult-child's type of alternative lifestyle originate?" "Are my ideas a reflection of my own sense of the present situation, or are they simply a set of beliefs and viewpoints that I have picked up along the way?" "How do these stereotypes influence my relationship with my adult-child?" and, "Do I want to continue to view the situation from the perspective of my present ideology, or would it be useful to adjust this perspective in some way?"

These or similar questions may naturally arise as you begin to examine the origins of your stereotypes. They can serve as guidelines to assist you in the process of learning to differentiate between your own ideas and those you have acquired through social and cultural conditioning. Through this process of discrimination, you may also discover that many of your opinions, worries and concerns about your adult-child are based on a set of pre-programmed beliefs, and not upon your own inherent capacity to accurately perceive and understand the present reality. You may even find yourself beginning to accept values that differ from your own. Of course you should not abandon the views and values you have always adhered to, but you may gain a greater freedom to allow others to live according to their ideals and beliefs as well. One father who was concerned about the influence a guru was having on his son, reported the following:

> "I had a man-to-man talk with my son's guru. I was questioning him about the issue of power, and how too much power can turn even the best of people sour. He (the teacher) turned to me and said, 'You're absolutely right. It's a very tentative position. A teacher has to watch himself carefully every step of the way.' I must admit, I was impressed — maybe it was all right after all."

Are We All Brainwashed?: A Popular Stereotype

> "My mom and I were out to lunch. I can tell when there's something brewing in her. She started telling me how terrible the crisis at Waco was, and then asked, 'How is what you're doing different from cults like Waco?'

I turned to her and questioned, 'How is your church different from a cult?'

She got flustered and said, 'Well, if I don't do everything the minister says, I don't get kicked out.'

'Well,' I responded, 'We don't get kicked out either.'

'We don't have to give all our money to the church,' she continued. I told her that we didn't either. I further explained that we don't have arms and weapons, that we're not being brainwashed, and that we are free to come and go as we please. I understand her biases because they are so common in our culture, yet in another way it is so outrageous. What I am involved with is no different than the church, it's just not mainstream so it's labeled a cult."

The stereotypical belief that people who live alternative lifestyles are being brainwashed, or unduly influenced by their group or its leaders, is one of the most commonly misconstrued ideas about alternative lifestyles. Of course, in a small minority of circumstances this *is* the case. However, in placing energy and attention on the degree to which one's adult-child is being influenced by others, the parent is ignoring the fact that *all people* are subjected to the influences of the particular culture to which they belong — be it from their religious ministers, their politicians, their bosses or even many popular sports or entertainment figures.

Although a parent may be greatly concerned about the degree to which his adult-child appears to be under the influence of a given teacher, group identity or philosophy, the parent needs to be honest about the fact that he, too, is influenced by *his* religious leaders or philosophy, or by the culture to which he belongs. In some cases the only difference is that one set of ideologies or leaders are agreed on by the majority of a culture, and the other is agreed on only by a minority. At first glance, it is easy to hypoth-esize that those beliefs held by the majority have come to be so because they are the "right" beliefs, or that they represent true in-tegrity and wisdom. However, there are many historical events and trends that suggest otherwise.

By virtue of Adolph Hitler's immense personal power and charisma — qualities that are equally as common to spiritual lead-ers as they are to presidents and CEO's — he convinced the mass-es of German people that Jews (as well as Gypsies, homosexuals, and even philosophers and artists) were evil and deserved to be slaughtered. One would like to think that the people who were influenced by Hitler were foolish and ignorant, but in fact they were ordinary people like us — including many professionals, people of wealth and education, artists and diplomats.

Similarly, in the case of Vietnam, most Americans never knew what the war was about. They assumed that the President and the Department of Defense, as representatives of democracy, were making responsible and intelligent decisions, and by means of their tax dollars, the public consented to the influence of their leaders.

Television is yet another enormous influence on the attitudes, preferences, and biases of the people in a given culture. Viewers are constantly being presented with specific ideas about how women should be (skinny, blond, sexy, submissive, young), and how men should be (muscular, suave, strong, invulnerable, wealthy). Commercials are continuously sending overt and sub-liminal messages about what type of soap a person should use to make themselves most attractive, what kinds of food will bring them joy, and what brand of car will make them most noticeable. This type of "conditioning" creates a certain uniformity within a culture that is not necessarily expressive of an individual's uniqueness or essence. Yet, like most forms of conditioning, it is so subtle and pervasive that when you reach out to buy Ivory™ soap in the supermarket, instead of Dove™, you are probably not making a conscious connection between your preference and the images of cliffs, oceans and trees that you saw on the soap commercial the day before.

Everybody is in fact already being influenced to one degree or another. Individuals must discern for themselves which influences are beneficial to them and which are harmful. Becoming aware that we are being influenced is what provides us with the ability to distinguish the difference between the two.

The Paradigm

Science explains the process we use to construct our worldview, and the way we resist any alteration or change to it, by offering the concept of the *paradigm*. A paradigm is a model or worldview consisting of a set of preconceived notions into which we categorize the constant flow of data and stimuli that enter our field of experience. There are also cultural paradigms — those worldviews and ways of perceiving reality that are understood and adhered to by the members of a given culture. When incoming information or data does not comply with the criteria of our already-existing paradigm, we either reject or otherwise distort the information in order to preserve our present paradigm, or we allow the incoming data to instigate a restructuring of the paradigm.

An adult-child's choice to pursue an alternative lifestyle is an example of a situation in which a parent's paradigm may be challenged by a set of incoming data that does not correspond to her already existing worldview. The easier option for the parent is to reject the incoming data — "I don't want to hear about it." A parent may simply pretend to herself that nothing has changed — continuing to send boxes of cookies even though her son has stated that he is no longer eating sugar; or continuing to inquire if her daughter intends to go to medical school . . . long after her daughter's formal education has ended. Parents can discard the incoming data in a multitude of ways — overtly through an outright verbal rejection of the adult-child's lifestyle, or subtly, by insisting to herself that her adult-child is simply "going through a phase."

Generally speaking, we don't want to restructure our paradigms — doing so implies the dissolution of an entire set of assumptions and beliefs, often unconscious, that have formulated our worldview. Although ultimately this dissolution may give birth to a model that is much wider and freer, nonetheless the process of dissolution is frequently painful or uncomfortable. We often lose the perspective that we are in transition. If, at this point, we become fearful about what is happening, we may revert back to our original paradigm — for although it may have been limited, it was somehow safe and predictable. (It is not that we are necessarily *conscious* of this process. If the possibility for the shift into a wider worldview was as easy as simply wishing it, everybody would be in that state. Instead, the processes described here more often occurs automatically and unconsciously.)

This process of shifting paradigms can, however, be brought into consciousness. Such a shift requires our willingness to literally open ourselves up to what may be an entirely new set of ideas or beliefs. Understand, however, that changing your paradigm does not imply that you must in any way "convert" to a new lifestyle or ideology. Instead, it involves expanding or opening your mind, and thereby your heart. If the form and activities of your life *do* change as a result of this shift in paradigm, they will change organically of their own accord, and will in no way be forced or unnatural.

A shift in paradigm does not usually result from merely thinking that we should change our worldview. Instead, a change of lasting value is the result of investigating our existing paradigm, i.e, asking ourselves, somewhat relentlessly, whether or not our worldview is broad enough to honor the beliefs and practices of diverse cultures and subcultures throughout the world. In so doing, we gain the necessary clarity and courage to face the pain of our own small-mindedness or small-heartedness. When this occurs, a shift to a healthier and more encompassing paradigm will arise of its own accord.

When an adult-child chooses to live an alternative lifestyle, the parent's willingness to allow her paradigm to shift is unlikely to result in any change in her own lifestyle. Rather, it will manifest as a greater openness to accept and honor both her adult-child and his choice of lifestyle.

A Reflection on the Diversity of Cultures

"In the Chinese culture into which I was born, there is an important Confucian idea of 'filial piety'. Many other cultures have similar values—with parents wanting their children to take care of them when they get older, but in Chinese families this is a very strong injunction.

One day, fifteen years after I had moved away from home to join a religious community, my parents said to me, 'Remember that you're Chinese. Don't forget your family — your mother and your father; you are still Chinese.' Their urging that I go back to live with them has always been there — every time I speak to them over the phone they ask me about it; this issue has been long-standing since the day I left home. There's no real acknowledgement that I may be involved in something important to me, and that I wouldn't just pick up and leave at any moment. I don't think they'll ever understand."

We can gain a clearer and more objective understanding of the factors which contribute to the creation of any given culture by considering many different cultures around the world. Many Americans, however, have been conditioned from childhood into the stereotypical belief that America and the countries of Europe are the only civilized countries, and that the rest of the world is underdeveloped and unsophisticated. As a result of this bias, the values and practices of the people in these cultures tend to be discounted, by all but the anthropologists, as a valuable resource of knowledge. This stereotype tends to be unconscious. If it were consciously examined, it would be obvious that the four billion or so individuals that comprise the non-Western world are not backward, unintelligent and unsophisticated.

Cultures around the world live in tremendous health, harmony and well-being while practicing a multitude of religions, rituals, art forms and methods of childraising. Together, these practices constitute the form in which the individuals in that culture carry out the tasks of their daily lives. Environment, socioeconomic structure, standard of living, religious foundation . . . these elements all contribute to the creation of any given culture. For example, the Bribri, indigenous people of Costa Rica, have developed a rich tradition of oral history due in part to the fact that there is no electric lighting in the rainforest they inhabit. Therefore, every evening is spent engaged in sharing stories by candlelight. In India, where a belief in God is woven into all of life's activities, a stranger will be fed a meal in almost any home due to the belief that serving another human being is one way in which an individual can serve God. Similarly, the fast-food culture in America has emerged as a response to the needs of people who are leading rapidly-paced lives that do not allot them the necessary time required for extensive food preparation.

The point of this consideration is neither to imply that contemporary western culture is in any way bad or wrong nor that other more "exotic" cultures are good or right, but instead to remind the reader that there are many "right" ways to live.

As we've noted many times before, just because your adult-child's lifestyle is different, it doesn't mean it's bad. One helpful perspective from which to view alternative communities and lifestyles is to see them as distinct cultures in and of themselves — each with a set of ideologies, practices, and ways of approaching daily life that are markedly different from those of the surrounding culture.

"I don't think that there are easy answers for parents whose children have chosen lifestyles that are so different from the surrounding culture, even in a case like mine when my parents had raised me talking leftist politics over dinner and going to rallies and marches for all kinds of social issues. Particularly in the case of spiritually-based alternative communities such as ashrams or meditation centers, there is so little precedent or understanding of real spiritual focus in our culture. We don't live in a culture in which it is not only common, but also highly respected, for a seventeen-year-old boy or girl to leave home and pursue spiritual life as a monk or a nun."

Parents may have great difficulty in accepting their adult-child's choice to live according to principles and practices that are outside of contemporary mainstream culture. However, an examination of other cultures and the ways in which they successfully carry out sophisticated and well-balanced lives, combined with the recognition that alternative lifestyles represent viable subcultures (as opposed to counter-cultures) within a larger culture, may help the parent to realize that his adult-child is operating according to a different set of cultural norms that are neither right nor wrong in essence, but are instead chosen intentionally in order to create a culture that will most optimally fulfill the needs of a given group of people. Whether those ideologies and practices embraced by any culture are in fact the best possible choices cannot be judged. "Culture" is not a stagnant entity, but rather a constantly evolving set of ways in which human beings relate to their lives and circumstances.

It is helpful to understand the depth to which your perspective about your adult-child's lifestyle is influenced by cultural and social influences as described in this chapter, as well as the psychological issues that were raised in the previous one. Nonetheless, understanding is only the beginning. You may or may not be able to actively integrate this information into your life without help of some sort. You are not weak because you turn toward external help. The following chapter sets forth a thorough inventory of the available resources that you can use for assistance — ranging from your family and friends, to licensed psychotherapists — and the advantages and disadvantages of each.

8.

Sources of Help

"I didn't know where to turn when my daughter decided to have a completely unconventional wedding ceremony . . . in the woods, no less; she also determined to keep her maiden name. I was deeply disappointed, and confused. I went to my minister and talked to him about it. He was very compassionate with my pain, but also shared that he had three kids of his own and not only did he understand, but he had seen much worse. He told me an interesting thing too . . . that in the old days in England a woman always kept her own name and added her husband's on to it. Just hearing this from him gave me some sense of reassurance."

Finding out that your adult-child, sibling, grandchild or close friend has chosen to lead an alternative lifestyle is often an event that is marked by challenges. These challenges may feel immense to you and there is no reason for you to traverse this seemingly unmapped territory alone. It is natural and useful for you to consider turning to outside help during this period.

In fact, however, the territory is *not* new. Many parents have come face-to-face with the same dilemmas that you are now encountering and have emerged from them successfully and with a sense of greater wholeness. Many more parents, counselors and professionals are able to understand and empathize with various aspects of your experience, and to assist you in sorting out your thoughts, clarifying your emotions, experiencing your feelings and learning how to interact with your adult-child anew. This chapter discusses the reasons for which you might turn toward external

134 When Sons and Daughters Choose Alternate Lifestyles

help at this time, and lists the resources that you can turn to for this assistance.

When you are considering the most useful source of help, keep in mind that you want someone who will assist you in unraveling *your own* thoughts and feelings about the issues. In a state of confusion or uncertainty, people commonly turn to those who will provide them with concrete advice . . . sometimes even telling them exactly what to do. Unfortunately, too many "helpers" are ready and willing to do just that, and far too few actually possess the clarity and integrity to do so.

Sometimes, all you need is someone to listen to you. So much may be going on inside your mind that you just need to talk in order to sort things out. At other times, you simply want a safe space in which to express your feelings.

Choose a source of help that is attuned to your specific needs in this particular situation, and not one that operates by any set formula or agenda. No two individuals or situations are alike, and an effective response depends entirely upon the needs of the circumstance. You need help only in order to extrapolate your own self-knowledge and to unravel the ongoing questions that arise for you. The clarity you discover within yourself will automatically provide you with the most accurate knowledge about how to carry on in your situation.

It is O.K. to Ask for Help

Everybody needs help. *Getting help does not indicate that there is something wrong with you.* In fact, one sign of mental and emotional sanity is when a person can acknowledge the need for external assistance. Particularly during times of crises or intense emotional stress, we lose the capacity to view our lives with clarity and accuracy. We simply need to turn to someone else.

Strong cultural precedents, however, weigh heavily against this natural need for support. Men are taught not to feel and not to need — they are told that their job is to provide financial security to their families and to be strong, sturdy and without emotion. Women, especially in modern times, have begun to feel the need to be equally strong and independent, withholding signs of vulnerability lest these be interpreted as weakness.

To make matters worse, a particularly pervasive cultural belief about psychotherapy and counseling says that if an individual seeks this type of help, he or she has definite "mental problems," or is somehow "sick." Although this attitude is slowly changing, a strong stigma remains around the pursuit of professional help — even when one seeks this help to gain greater self-knowledge or clarity.

Historically, until very recently, all cultures were centered around community living, with built-in systems of help and support. Women spent a great deal of time with other women in the course of their daily tasks and would naturally share their questions and concerns. Similarly, men engaged in activities that provided a sense of comradery, allowing them to feel bonded to and supported by each other. Only in the past several decades has society become fast-paced . . . have single-parent and nuclear families grown up in isolation from their larger families . . . have organic support systems broken down. In contemporary Western culture, professional counseling or psychotherapy is often the only available source of reliable help to the struggling individual Whether we turn to a therapist, to a spiritual or religious leader, or to a spouse or friend, we should remember that our need for help is completely natural — an expression of our relatedness with humanity, and a testimony to the common pain we bear.

Sources of Help

For some of you, this may be the first time that you have sought assistance. You may not know where to begin. If so, you need not be discouraged. Reliable help is available — your only job will be to practice attention and discrimination when choosing whose "hand to hold." This section lists the various resources that are available, and specific considerations to keep in mind when pursuing these sources. A particularly detailed description of the various types of professional counseling is offered, not because this is necessarily the best source of help, but because many people are unfamiliar with the distinctions among these approaches.

*Parents Who Have Been Through It

Although all of the following resources may be of value to you, there is often no better source of help than other parents who have adult-children who have chosen to live alternative lifestyles; parents who are intimately familiar with the depth and complexity of the issues surrounding this circumstance and, ideally, those who have successfully moved into healthy, supportive and loving relationships with their adult-children. The key word here is "successfully," as there are many parents who have had their adult-children kidnapped or deprogrammed, or who have otherwise persuaded them from their chosen lifestyle, who are all-too-eager to share their opinions and strategies with other parents who are going through this process.

Only those parents who have been through this and have maintained or come back into loving relationship with their adult-children will be able to speak from actual experience. Do not be discouraged, however, if you cannot at first locate such parents. They may be difficult to find. Sometimes you will discover that your counselor, priest or acquaintance has been through similar trials, or that they can give you names of other parents who have.

*Licensed and Non-Licensed Psychiatrists, Psychotherapists, Therapists, and Counselors:

Aside from psychiatrists, whose licensure is standard throughout the country, the qualifications necessary to become a licensed counselor or therapist vary from state to state. You may need to know if your psychotherapist or counselor is licensed, particularly if you want your treatment covered by insurance; however, there are many good counselors who are not officially certified, and many poor ones who have full accreditation and years of experience. Your best source of guidance in this case is whether or not the individual has been referred to you by someone who you know and whose opinion you value, as well as your own feeling about the counselor or therapist.

It is perfectly appropriate to "check out" a therapist or counselor for one or two initial sessions in order to get a "feel" for him or her. Some therapists and counselors give an initial "interview" free of charge, whereas others will charge full or partial fee for the first session. It is fine to ask. Beyond the first sessions, however, once you make a choice try to stick with it. Once engaged in this therapy you will be challenged in various ways. Quite commonly, people come up against a certain resistance in themselves and then unconsciously attempt to blame or criticize the therapist for this, as a way of avoiding a confrontation about the real issue. The time to terminate therapy is rarely the point at which you are fed up or angry with the therapist. On the contrary, that is the time to stick it out. Therapy usually ends when you have a strong, clear, and grounded sense that you have completed what *you* needed to do; or when you recognize that your particular therapist is unable to take you beyond a certain point that you need to go.

If professional therapy or counseling is a new endeavor for you, you should know that you can talk to your therapist about *anything*, including your concerns and doubts about the therapist himself. Depending upon the orientation of the therapist, he may or may not respond to this directly; what is important, however, is that you feel the freedom to share with him whatever you need to.

Psychiatrists: Psychiatrists are medical doctors who specialize in treating mental/emotional issues. What distinguishes psychiatrists from other practitioners in the helping profession is that they are authorized to prescribe medications to treat various conditions. Except as needed in specific cases, medications serve to buffer and cover the individual's emotions, and in doing so provide little resolution for the underlying issues.

Licensed Psychologists, Psychotherapists and Counselors: There are many different titles that indicate that an individual is licensed in the field of psychology or counseling, and the way in which these titles are used varies from state to state. In general, these individuals have acquired either a Master's or a Ph.D. degree in the field of psychology or counseling, have completed an extensive internship, and have passed a state examination. Although the quality of help will vary significantly from counselor to counselor, you might start here in seeking professional help. Lacking a referral, check your phone book for listings. Most licensed therapists will indicate their qualifications in their ad.

Non-licensed therapists and counselors: Often practicing under the same titles as those listed above, these individuals have not been state certified. However, many of these people have undergraduate and graduate degrees and have done extensive field work and internships, and for various reasons have opted not to get state certification. There are excellent helping professionals available that fall into this category. Others are under-qualified and are practicing under a title that does not reflect their capabilities. If you choose to seek professional help from a licensed or non-licensed therapist or counselor, there are two avenues by which to proceed. *Brief-therapy* and counseling is becoming more popular due to the financial demands of professional help. This type of counseling lasts anywhere from one to twelve sessions and is focused on one particular issue or problem. However, even in brief therapy do not be surprised if you are asked to examine certain issues from your past or present that do not seem directly related to the primary problem for which you seek assistance. In cases of one's adult-child choosing to live an alternative lifestyle, it is rarely the circumstance itself that is the sole cause of your pain or concern. Long-term therapy, which may last anywhere from a few months to a few years, tends to go much deeper into the underlying feelings and sources of your dilemma and will provide you with an opportunity to gain a more profound understanding of many aspects of your life, in addition to your relationship with your adult-child.

Lay-Professionals

This group includes ministers and rabbis, social workers and peer-counselors who work on crises telephone lines. When turning to this source of help, it is important to use your judgment in deciding who can best assist you at this time. Just because someone is a minister does not mean that he or she can provide you with what you need. On the other hand, a trusted priest or social worker may be able to offer you invaluable guidance. You own capacity for discernment is essential in this case, as in all others.

Support Groups

Multitudes of support groups are available in larger cities and even in small towns. These groups range from nationally known "12-Step" programs, to groups who gather to discuss a specific issue (i.e., meetings designed specifically for parents whose adult-children have chosen to live alternative lifestyles), to gatherings of men and women who meet informally for the purpose of supporting one another. Again, the value of this form of help varies from group to group and only you will be able to know if you have found the appropriate group for you through your own experimentation. Ask around to get referrals from a trusted source. The particular benefit of 12-Step programs is both that they are nationally known, and that they value the need for individuals to express themselves without being given feedback or advice unless they ask for it. If you choose to investigate this resource, you will discover that there are many types of 12-Step groups available, ranging from Codependent's Anonymous (CODA) to Alcoholic's Anonymous (AA), and that there are further differences between the various groups that deal with a specific issue depending upon the facilitator and the members. CODA is a good place to begin when pursuing this option, both because codependency tends to be common among most parents who experience marked difficulties due to their adult-child's choice to live an alternative lifestyle, and because the group is open to individuals who are dealing with a wide range of circumstances. Furthermore, it is not necessary to sign up for these groups — you can come and go as you please.

*Spouses/Intimate Partners

Inevitably, if you have concerns or are experiencing difficulties related to your adult-child's choice to live an alternative lifestyle you will find yourself turning to your spouse or mate if you have one. However, there is a distinction between turning to him or her in search of validation for your opinions and worries, or as a place in which to wager your complaints about your adult-child, and turning to your spouse for clear and specific support. In the case of the former, though it may provide you with a certain type of temporary relief, you will obtain no lasting value. In the case of the later, he or she may be able to provide you with a valuable source of support and feedback.

Is your partner able to listen to you in an attentive, nonjudgmental way, and to give you helpful feedback? What particular position does your partner take on this issue? Does your partner have an investment in you taking a specific stance in the given situation (i.e., if he or she has a strong bias against all cults, will he be able to really listen to you or to provide you with the objectivity that you need in order to elicit your own sense of the situation)? Realizing that your spouse or partner is not necessarily the best source of support in this situation does not imply that he or she is not an excellent partner — even a wonderful partner cannot and should not provide for all your needs. Often, because of differences between the sexes, women find it useful to turn to other women, and men to turn to other men in times of need.

The support that you are able to receive from a spouse or partner will also be dependent upon the way in which you approach him or her. If you approach the other in a mood of self-pity, you are likely to get sympathy; if you approach with a certain conviction about your perspective, your partner is likely to agree with you. However, if you simply let your partner know that you are in need of someone to listen to you, to provide you with clear and honest feedback (if this is what you want), to give you a "reality check," or simply for some nurturing, you are likely to elicit that, if it is within your partner's capacity to do so.

Friends and Relatives
    Friends and relatives can be an invaluable source of support. If you are concerned with a specific friend or relative's opinions and judgements of either you or your adult-child's lifestyle, he or she will not be a useful source of support. In general, the criteria to consider when discerning if a particular friend or relative will be a helpful source of support is similar to that which is involved in assessing the ability of a partner or spouse's capacity to support you (See Spouses/Intimate Partners above). Just because someone is a good friend or a close relative does not mean that he or she is a reliable source of support. Sometimes friends and relatives who are slightly more distant and less involved in your immediate circumstances will be better able to help you. Again, this varies from friend to friend, and relative to relative. (See the next chapter, *Talking with Friends and Relatives.*)

Caution: Be Aware of Biased Sources of Help

    Subtle and unconscious dynamics may be at play within the person who is seeking support, and it is useful for you to be attentive to this so that you may avoid falling into this trap. As referred to previously, when the mind is clouded by fear and anxiety, it will often shape your experience to coincide with your fears, and then encourage you to seek sources of support that will validate the reality of your fear. If you have a strong enough conviction about a certain idea or concern, you will "see" what you fear, regardless of the reality of the circumstance. For example, an individual who is afraid of snakes will see every piece of rope along the road as a snake. Likewise, if a parent suspects that her adult-child is in a destructive cult, she will be vigilant to any and all signs of this. Information that has nothing to do with cults or presents no sign of danger to her adult-child will be interpreted as evidence of the destructiveness of his group. If this parent seeks external support, and if her fears are strong enough, she is likely to turn to those sources that will confirm the credibility of her fears. For example, a parent who believes that her adult-child is being manipulated or brainwashed by the leader of his group may turn to a source of "support," such as an "expert" on cults, who will validate and even encourage her deepest fears. Or, a parent who believes that her peace of mind has been ruined due to her adult-child's decision to lead an alternative lifestyle may find a therapist who is knowledgeable about the ways in which parents' lives are ruined when their children join cults, and who is able to "empathize" with her situation. The words "support" and "empathize" are placed in quotations because it is not in fact genuine support or empathy that the parent is receiving, but instead a biased perspective cloaked in the guise of objective assistance.

As is discussed throughout the book, alternative lifestyles are a strongly charged subject about which few people are objective. Some groups which claim to offer "help" to those dealing with these issues expound the same prejudices and zealous attitudes against alternative lifestyles that they accuse the cults of embodying. Just because a group claims to specialize in this area, or because an individual calls himself an expert about this issue, is no guarantee that the group or person is an objective and reliable source of support. If a parent is not careful, she may find herself in the hands of a so-called professional who will simply confirm her fears and doubts, whatever they may be. Effective counseling or support does not usually give directive advice — instead it provides you with a caring and supportive environment that enables you to sort through and clarify your own reactions, perceptions and feelings, and to make decisions that are based in this knowledge.

If you find that your sources of support are in fact biased, don't be alarmed. This frequently results in a society in which there is a shared apprehension about cults and alternative life-styles. Forewarned is forearmed. You are sensitizing yourself to these potential pitfalls and are therefore less likely to be further influenced by them.

Where Not To Turn

The one place you should not turn for support is to your adult-child. Understandably, you may want to turn to your adult-child at this time, particularly if you have a close relationship. After all, who better than your child may appreciate the pain you're going through? Unfortunately, this simply doesn't work. The emotions that you and your adult-child are likely to be facing during this period are intricately linked with one another, and the issues that each are facing are too closely intertwined for you to be able to support one another during this period. If you turn to your adult-child for support at this time, you are beckoning drama and difficulty into your life. If you pour the pain you feel onto your adult-child, you are pulling on any codependent tendencies he or she might have to feel guilty or somehow responsible for your pain. Admittedly, parent and adult-child are both in this situation together — but the goal for each should be the freedom of, not codependency with, the other. Each must find a way to be in relationship that supports this aim.

This is by no means to say that you and your adult-child should not have contact with each other. Instead, it is a reminder that the relationship between them you likely to be in a state of transformation during this period, and it is wise for you to use sensitivity and be clear in your intentions when interacting with your adult-child. Real support at this time means finding an objective and compassionate source of help for yourself, and supporting your adult-child by allowing him or her to do the same.

Self-Support

Some of us may be unable to reach out for help even when we know we need it. Support is almost always available, even though it may not seem that way if we have never allowed ourselves to be helped emotionally or psychologically. Some people simply aren't ready, or simply don't want to involve others in their concerns — and that is all right. Nonetheless, even for those who do find effective sources of help, there is no substitute for on-going self-support. Self-support means that you become your own ally in the present situation. In times of difficulty, we easily turn against ourselves. Although externally we may be defending our perspective, and even if our words are backed with confidence, internally we may be faced with a war in which we are playing both sides, restlessly moving from camp to camp in our fear and confusion.

The need for self-support calls on us to discover compassion for ourselves and the ability to nurture ourselves. Compassion arises from a deep understanding of the complexity and difficulty of the predicament as a whole, or when we finally realize that we cannot afford to be uncompassionate — that the costs of a lack of love are just too high. Compassion for oneself is the process of directing love inward, which in no way excludes the directing of love outward, for love is not scarce. When we discover love for ourselves, we will find an abundance of love that will naturally pour forth from us and extend to all those around us.

For many people, true compassion for themselves is simply not their reality, and there is no point in fooling themselves about this. Many of us were raised in environments in which, although our parents loved us in the best way they knew how, we still grew up feeling unloved. If we felt unloved as a child we will automatically draw the conclusion that we are essentially unlovable. For many of us, compassion for ourselves must be cultivated and allowed to grow.

As a parent, you can cultivate self-compassion by learning to nurture yourself and by providing yourself with love and understanding. You can begin simply by setting aside time to pay attention to those issues and feelings which are most true for you at the present time (See Chapter 3: *It's All About Grief; Where to Begin*). If you like to walk . . . around the park . . . by the water . . . in the mountains, why not purposefully set aside time to do this? If like so many of us, you tend to get "stressed out" due to overwork, make an agreement with yourself that this week you will spend one evening at home, doing things that are calming and soothing, and are unrelated to your work. You know how your bodily health and mental health are connected. Remember that every time you make a choice in favor of eating good food, breathing clean air, taking time to connect with yourself . . . you are being compassionate with yourself. No matter how you decide to begin to nurture yourself, what is important is that you begin something. Set the intention to do so and then follow through. With each tiny step you send yourself a direct message that you *are* lovable . . . that you deserve to be treated with compassion. By providing yourself with a source of clear and consistent nurturance over a period of time, you nourish the ground in which love and a capacity for genuine self-support will eventually grow and flourish.

Another way to nourish yourself is by providing love and compassion to others. (Ideally, such "love" is not motivated by guilt, obligation, or the wish for this love to be returned. But even so, we can't wait until our love is 100% pure and selfless before offering it to others.) When you feel a lack of love within yourself, if you turn to help another person in some way, love itself is drawn forth from within you, benefitting you and the one who you are loving.

Many people find keeping a journal to be a valuable aid in self-reflection and self-support, while others take refuge in a certain piece of prose or a particular musical composition in order to restore balance within themselves. Only you know what works best for you.

Whether or not you have turned to a psychotherapist, a spouse or a friend for help at this time, there is no substitute for self-support. All other forms of support are useful, and at times may even be essential, but it is you who must live with yourself moment to moment. Only you have the capacity to draw forth the love that is needed to transform your experience. All sources of external support serve to illustrate and point to that love and compassion that already exist within you.

Becoming familiar with the sources of help available, and pursuing them as necessary, marks the last segment in the "middle phase" in which parents undertake a process of self-exploration and education in order to understand the way in which their personal psychology as well as cultural influences color the lens through which they view their son's or daughter's lifestyle.

III. The New Beginning — Integration

The initial phase of learning about an adult-child's choice to lead an alternative lifestyle is marked by simply learning to cope with the new set of circumstances. This is the time when parents may have to deal with feelings of shock and loss, while simultaneously making the choice to relate with their adult-child based on their underlying love and respect for him or her as an individual.

9.

$\mathcal{H}$ow to Support
When You Don't Agree

"I was in a gay relationship and affiliated with the German branch of an international commune — a parent's nightmare! One time when I was visiting my boyfriend's parents, his father and I went out for a smoke. He asked me about our lives and about the community we were involved in . . . about the finances, the belief system. I could tell it was difficult for him to understand, but he really tried to listen.

The next time we went for a visit and he and I were outside for a smoke, he said to me, 'I've been collecting silver coins for twenty-five years. It's not much, but do you want to sell them to support your business?' He wanted to give his share to our relationship. It was a nice gesture, as I know he doesn't really approve of our relationship. It's not so common when you're in a gay relationship for parents to be that accepting."

Agreement is not equal to love, just as disagreement is not equal to lack of love. Likewise, you can completely understand another person while not agreeing with what he or she says or does. Although we usually want agreement, the capacity to support another — to stand behind him or her as an individual no matter what he does — is neither contingent upon our agreement with the choices that he makes, nor our capacity to understand the whole of his perspective.

Not uncommonly, after learning about our adult-child's life and speaking with him or her extensively about this, we may still be faced with the fact that we do not agree with our adult-child's choices. Nonetheless, having established some distance from the initial feelings of panic and uncertainty, we generally want to find some way to express our ongoing love. At this point, we may find ourselves amid a genuine dilemma — uncertain how to respond. However, if a balanced, compassionate approach is cultivated, this need not be a problem. When we ask ourselves the question, "Even if I don't agree with my adult-child's choices, am I willing to sacrifice my relationship with her because of this?," we uncover the root of the dilemma. Philosophical and ideological agreement with one's adult-child are by no means a prerequisite for relationship; a genuine wish to know and honor our adult-child is. We are being asked to place the foundation for relationship — unconditional love, genuine respect and support for our adult-child — above and beyond the question of agreement or disagreement. At this point we must say to ourselves, "No matter how my adult-child chooses to live her life, and no matter my feelings about it, we are still family. My allegiance lies with my adult-child, whatever path she chooses to follow."

Jerry, whose twenty-one-year-old daughter is the singer in a rock band, put it this way:

> "There are parents who educate themselves about their child's lifestyle and still don't agree with it. They feel like their child has betrayed them, though there is no evidence of this. It seems like there are those parents who are given the information and whether they agree with it or not stay in loving relationship with their children, and there are those parents who don't, or who stay in a relationship that is superficial and aggressive. It is up to the parent."

Love In Action

Particularly in times of crises among family members, love is expressed best through action. As a parent, you might be saying to yourself, "My child knows that I love him no matter what." But are you sure this is so? Look closely at the way in which you interact with him. Are your conversations with him loving interactions, or are they carefully disguised arguments and debates cloaked in kind words? Do your gestures toward him reflect your care for him, or are they designed to manipulate the situation in some way? Do you tend to relate to one another with mutual honor and interest, or with disrespect and disdain? Particularly in times of tension and disagreement, people often act unloving toward one another.

Love in action is expressed in very basic ways. You may make a conscious choice not to argue with your adult-child about philosophical differences, even though you may have to literally hold yourself back from doing so. It may consist of you actually telling your adult-child, "I love you" if you have not told him this in a long time. You may choose to say to her, "Irrespective of my opinion about your lifestyle, I firmly support you in following your own unique path." Making eye contact and carefully considering what she is saying when you speak with her in person is a great way to express your love. Love in action could consist of you reading the literature she sends you about her community or chosen lifestyle — or may mean that you pay careful attention to the boundaries she makes, such as not sending her Christmas cards, or not trying to make her feel guilty if she only calls every six weeks. Sending her flowers or kind letters, or taking her out to her favorite restaurant when she comes to visit you are specific ways of expressing your love.

Essentially, you give your adult-child what you can. You love her in whatever ways you are able. If the only thing you are able to do is send her a ten dollar check on her birthday, that's what you do; if you are able to give her your full emotional support, you do that.

Acting As If

A useful tool for putting love into action is the practice of *acting as if* you support and respect your adult-child. Simply put, you tell yourself that you support your son or daughter wholly, and you approach all aspects of your relationship with her from the basis of that premise. Contrary to the idea that *acting as if* is somehow superficial or untruthful because you are not actually *feeling* supportive of your adult-child at that moment, this powerful and profound technique actually addresses the *essential* truth of your relationship — the truth that underlies the mutual defensiveness, opinionated debates and futile attempts to change one another that characterize non-supportive relationships. Your loving support is an expression of the truth, and the disagreement and lack of support are much more an expression of falseness and superficiality in the relationship.

The *acting as if* practice is done by focusing your attention on your adult-child himself instead of on his choices. You focus on his positive qualities and on the love that you feel for him. In doing so, you are reminding yourself that it is your adult-child that you wish to support, as opposed to your own ideas and opinions.

Practically speaking, *acting as if* may involve you holding back from sharing your judgements and criticisms of his lifestyle when you speak to him, and instead intentionally finding something positive to say about what he is doing. *Acting as if* may even mean supporting his current endeavors in some reasonable way — be it financially, or by helping him to collect information he may need, or by honoring his requests of you — even if within yourself you feel somewhat wary about their value, or suspect that his ventures will fail. You *act as if* based on the premise that you *do* support him, although you may not feel it — now or ever. Nevertheless, while you are struggling with your feelings you still want to convey to him a gesture of acknowledgement. If he feels the sincerity of your gesture, he is much more likely to express his own feelings of gratitude and respect for you as his parent. He may furthermore appreciate your willingness to hold back your own opinions in favor of being sensitive to his.

Refrain from the temptation to draw rapid conclusions about the value of *acting as if* you support your adult-child. Instead, just try it. You may discover to your amazement that not a moment of loving and supportive action is wasted. As you continue to practice *acting as if*, you may find that you are filled with greater love and appreciation within yourself, perhaps the greatest reward of *acting as if* you support your adult-child.

Even if this approach feels awkward or insincere, and even if you feel like biting your tongue every time you talk with your adult-child, you may find that if you keep doing it, one day your *acting as if* may evolve into genuine support. At this point you will be able to take an assessment of your relationship with your adult-child and see that it has changed — for the better!

If You Don't Want to Know, Don't Ask!

Until you are ready to support your son or daughter in another way, you may need to decide not to ask about those aspects of his or her lifestyle that you are unable to hear . . . those things that will disturb you, incite your reactivity and result in creating further distance in the relationship between you.

If you don't want to know, don't ask is an invitation for you to remember your larger intention to support your adult-child, and within this to make specific choices as to how you can best do this. *If you don't want to know, don't ask* suggests that sometimes the best way a parent can support his adult-child is to refrain from expressing interest on one level in the service of maintaining a sense of overall harmony and respect. Amrita, a forty-two-year-old mother who lives with her husband and two children at a residential retreat center, shares her story:

> "I've been a part of the community for twenty-one years and my mother still believes this is a

phase I'm going through. She doesn't mention
it. She won't call here for fear that a stranger
will answer the phone and she wouldn't know
what name to use. I know what she's going
through, so when we're together — even if it is
only once every four or five years — or when
we speak on the phone, we just don't talk about
it. We talk about everything else except what I
am up to — that's her measure of safety, her
area of protection, and I have to honor that."

A parent may discover what it is she really wants to know
about her adult-child's life by examining the motivations that underlie the questions she asks of him (See Chapter 4: *Approaching
Your Son or Daughter: Exploring Your Motivations*). For example,
a parent may find herself asking her adult-child about his guru because she thinks she is being polite and respectful to do so, whereas in fact she cannot stand to hear about his guru; or, she may ask
because she suspects that her son's teacher is manipulating him in
some way and she wants to investigate her suspicions. In both
cases, the parent may express this as though it is based in genuine
interest and curiosity; and in fact, if she has not examined her own
motivations, she herself may believe this is so. However, in both
of these cases it would be more appropriate for the parent not to
ask. A twenty-two-year-old English woman who is part of the
"Rave" movement, a post-modern counterculture, shares her sentiment:

"I'm starting to feel a warmth toward my parents when they don't ask me about certain parts
of my life because they know they can't handle
what I'm going to say. It's much better than
them asking for details they don't want to know
and then getting upset with what I say. The people who I hang out with are essentially good

people, but they do things my parents just
wouldn't understand such as taking certain
drugs and going to Rave dances. I used to think
they had to know everything about my life to
really support me, but I don't feel that way anymore. When they don't ask, it is a little bit more
superficial, but it's almost a loving gesture for
them to admit that they just can't hear it."

After a period of adjustment to the new circumstances of her
adult-child's life, the parent may in fact find herself genuinely
wondering who this teacher is who has moved her son so deeply,
or what this ideology is which her son is so passionate about. She
is aware that although she may be somewhat uneasy with what she
learns, she will be able to contain her reactions so as not to impede
her relationship with her son. Now the parent's motivations are
clear and her inquiries are supportive. Until this point, however,
her adult-child will likely appreciate that his parent is willing to
take responsibility for discerning what she is able to hear and what
she is not yet able to take in.

This approach does have limitations. If a parent chooses not
to know about her adult-child's lifestyle in the long run, if she
chooses not to know the way that he experiences his life and what
it is that is important to him, there will necessarily remain a gap of
understanding between them. Nevertheless, it is more important
that the parents ask about only as much as they can take, and still
remain open to relationship. If they attempt to take on more, they
may end up closing down in their relationship with their adult-
child, creating still further distance. Furthermore, a parent's decision not to ask more than she is able to accept and integrate at any
given time may serve as an intermediary stage that will allow for
the eventual unfolding of a relationship of genuine intimacy and
mutual respect.

Agreeing to Disagree

"Since I joined the convent, my conversation
with my parents is quite limited, as they are
atheists. I tell them, 'I've devoted my life to
God.' 'That's nice Michelle,' they respond,
'Are you sure there is one?!' "

There may come a point in the relationship between parent
and adult-child when they choose to make a conscious agreement
to disagree with one another. Whether this is stated outright or
whether it is mutually understood without words, an agreement to
disagree can be a strong and positive choice — for in acknowledging and accepting the fact of disagreement, there is actually agreement. The specific details of the disagreement are often subsumed
in the greater willingness to *agree to disagree* for the purpose of
maintaining overall harmony.

Agreeing to disagree should not be misinterpreted to mean
that it is all right to continue to argue, that it is O.K. to be stubborn
about one's point of view, or that an ongoing debate is what is
called for. Instead, an agreement to disagree means that the disa-
greements no longer need to be the focus, and that engaging discussions can take place about topics other than the ones that gen-
erate dissent and disagreement. The lack of agreement is not
being "swept under the carpet," but instead, when there is an agreement to disagree, both parent and adult-child choose to focus their
attention on one another in a way that neither indulges nor denies
their differences in opinion.

Recognize that there are various ways in which disagreement
is expressed between parent and adult-child. One way implies, "I
disagree with you because I think you are wrong, and in fact mis-
guided." Another way says, "I disagree with what you are saying,
as I see the situation quite differently." The distinctions in the
way disagreement is expressed are rarely stated directly, but are
instead implied in the tone, or the general mood in which parent

and adult-child relate with one another. In the former approach, the parent might say to her adult-child, "I can't understand why you are making these choices when you are so talented and have so many other options," whereas in the latter case she might say to him, "I don't see it that way, and I wouldn't choose the same for myself, but I respect your decision nonetheless."

It is surprising to discover how willing people are to remain in a state of disagreement, no matter how uncomfortable and destructive it is to their relationships, just to make a stand for their point of view — to prove that they are "right." Perhaps they fear that their perspective is proven invalid if they do not have the agreement of the other.

Even when a parent does not agree with the specifics of her adult-child's lifestyle choice, the basic underlying intention behind that choice can be respected. A parent can appreciate her adult-child's attempt to align his life according to the ideals he upholds. She can honor his intention to live a life of harmony. She can admire him for his willingness to take a great risk — a risk that is likely to be met with rejection and disapproval, not only by his parents but by society-at-large. Perhaps he will follow a certain path for a time and then come to realize that the choices he has made are not the best ones — so what?! The fact that he has had the courage and integrity to follow through with choices that are aligned with his highest ideals and aspirations is worthy of admiration in and of itself.

> "Things have changed over the past eighteen years. Now she tells me, 'I don't really approve of the way you live, but I know you're happy, and that's all I need to know. You're doing what you want and you love what you're doing and you love the people there."

The need to be, think or feel the same as the other is born out of a desire for union, or togetherness with the other, whereas differences in opinions or unique ideologies tend to magnify an underlying feeling of separation. However, separation and aloneness are not a function of uniqueness and difference. In fact, when the feeling of togetherness and connectedness is large enough to encompass individuality and uniqueness, the union that occurs is often greater than when there is agreement.

A parent who understands and recognizes his underlying wish for union and harmony, while at the same time realizing that his adult-child can and will make important decisions that differ from his wishes for her, will also realize that an agreement to disagree can create greater understanding in their relationship, and will allow his adult-child the space to be more fully herself. The relationship that results from this choice is one that is founded on the recognition of the wholeness and completeness of the situation *as it is.*

Agreeing to disagree means, "I'm O.K. You're O.K." It means that parent and adult-child are not the same and that this is O.K.!

When there is an agreement to disagree, interactions are no longer laced with the subtle forms of persuasion and coercion that so commonly characterize interchanges between parents and adult-children when there is strong disagreement about a central issue. One young woman who is deeply involved in the feminist movement elaborated on this point:

> "It was not my usual way of doing things. I had always been outspoken, ruthless, and insistent that my parents agree with my involvement in the feminist movement and my attendance at the annual women's musical festival. When I realized I could settle on the fact that we disagreed about the way that I chose to live my life, I found some surprising results. It was as if we had made an unspoken agreement not to speak about it. This was different than the unspoken

and unconscious agreements of childhood. This
agreement was conscious. It was based on the
mutual understanding that we were simply unable to agree about my lifestyle choices and that
we could not speak about it without an aggressive disagreement."

In many relationships that are loving, respectful and deeply
fulfilling to both the parents and their adult-child, the parents have
never agreed with their adult-child's lifestyle choice. Nevertheless, together they have decided to agree on the importance of relationship, love, and caring for one another, and in this way their
differences in opinion become insignificant.

Meeting on Common Ground

Meeting on common ground means that parents and their
adult-children recognize the shared ground they stand on in spite
of the differences in their approaches to life. They acknowledge
those areas of relationship in which they are most able to meet,
share, laugh and enjoy each other's company, as well as those are-
nas in which intimacy simply isn't possible, and they choose to intentionally engage their relationship in the areas in which they feel
most connected. When parents and their adult-children meet on
common ground, familiarity and connectedness allows them be
themselves, to relax and to appreciate one another. Becky, a former psychotherapist and mother of two children, articulates this
principle:

"The idea is to have relationship in the areas in
which relationship is possible. There are ways in
which my parents would like to understand me,
but they never will; and there are ways in which
we can really relate to and enjoy one another.
Parents should say to their kids, 'These are the

> areas where we're not in relationship and we
> don't need to try to be, and these are the areas in
> which we can really appreciate and understand
> each other, so let's meet there.' "

Common ground, on the most essential level, is discovered when we recognize the basic struggles that are shared among us by virtue of our humanness. We know that human beings grapple with the same issues in their desire to give and receive love, to find a way of life that makes them happy, to wind their way through the maze of emotions that arise in their day-to-day lives, and to make wise decisions. This understanding — that we're all in this together, that nobody *really* knows what is going on — and that although we all may act hurtful and uncaring at times, we do so only in an effort to protect ourselves from underlying feelings of vulnerability and fear, is our common ground of relatedness.

Practically, between you and your adult-child, common ground may refer to a particular place or activity. For example, you meet at a coffee house you both like, or go to the movies or a sporting event together. On an ideological or intellectual level, common ground indicates what types of conversations you can mutually engage in, or the topics of shared interest that you can both relate to. Still another layer of common ground is any emotional, philosophical and/or spiritual aspects of life which you both share. For example, you may discover that when you each talk about your personal philosophies on life that the relationship between you collapses, but when you cook a meal together or go for a walk, you are still able to connect with one another.

> "What seems to be healing is to talk about the
> things they are comfortable with in my life. I tell
> them about my Italian boyfriend, and they say,
> 'Oh, that's the most wonderful thing.' I talk
> about what they do care about. Why discuss all
> the things we disagree on when there are so

many things we like to talk about? I used to think it was necessary to be understood by my parents and for them to agree with what I was doing, but now I realize the value of accepting the limitations that exist, on my part as well as theirs, and focusing our attention on what we have. Things have gotten better and better."

When you and your adult-child accept the limitations that exist in your relationship, instead of clinging to the pain and disappointment that you feel because of them, you open up to the possibilities for more honest communication. Ironically, in accepting a given limitation, you have already moved beyond it. Thus, when you are willing to meet one another on common ground, you may discover that the ground you are standing on is much more solid and more expansive than you would have ever imagined.

Stepping Into Another Person's Shoes

The practice of stepping into another person's shoes will help you to recognize the commonalties between your own experiences and those of your adult-child, regardless of how different your circumstances may appear to be. Stepping into another person's shoes is the practice of empathy (See Chapter 4, *Approaching Your Son or Daughter: Essential Skill: Practice Empathy*).

When you choose to try on another person's "reality," you open yourself up to the full depth and range of his or her experience — including her struggles and her pain. You may recognize just how different her perception of reality is from yours. You might even touch upon a sense of your own aloneness — i.e., *nobody* else thinks or experiences life as you do. This insight, though initially disturbing, may lead to the recognition of existential aloneness as part and parcel of the human condition. Yet, in the realization that everyone is alone, you may find another aspect of our common ground of true understanding.

Imagination Exercise:

The following imagination exercise will allow you to step into your adult-child's shoes. Understanding the world from his or her point of view, you will have a better sense of where your perspectives cross paths, and whether or not you can meet her at these intersections. As you go through the following exercise, which can be done one or many times, allow yourself to adjust the details of the specific suggestions if this will enable you to access your adult-child's experience more clearly.

*Find a comfortable place to sit or lay down, and close your eyes. Take a few slow, deep breaths. Let yourself relax.

*Allow your adult-child to come into your mind — you may have an image of her, you may simply feel a sense of her or you may have a memory of her.

*Recall the love that fundamentally exists between you — perhaps remember a specific event, like the event of her birth, or a moment of joyful play with one another. Whether this memory reflects your present feelings for her or whether you must go back in time to access such a time is irrelevant.

*Now, begin to conjure a sense of what it is like for your adult-child in her new lifestyle. Imagine both the excitement and challenges that she may be facing. Consider what it is like for her to be making the choice to lead an alternative lifestyle in a society that does not support this. Contemplate what it might be like for her to share her experience with you, given your feelings. Allow yourself to get a sense of the courage it takes for her to make such a decision.

*Remembering the underlying intelligence and wisdom that is inherent in all humans, recognize that her decision was made for what she perceived to be good reasons — irrespective of whether or not you, as her parent, think they are the right ones.

*Consider the major decisions that you have made in your life. Think about times when you made strong choices to do what you had to in spite of the disapproval of others. Remember how you were treated at this time. What was helpful? What was hurtful? Continue to allow these types of considerations to pass through your mind. At this point you can guide yourself into further reflection about what your adult-child's present experience of her life may be like, and how it is for her to relate to you about this.

*When you feel ready to stop, gently open your eyes and return to your present reality. It is not important that you try to *do* anything with the information you have accessed; simply being willing to take in your adult-child's reality, and relating to her from a deeper awareness of her experience is a form of genuine support.

If you have come to learn how to support your adult-child, even when you don't agree with his or her choices, you have come a long way! However, it is likely that your relatives, close friends and other people whom you come into contact with on a daily basis are still laboring under the same stereotypes and biases that you were before going through this process. Talking with friends and relatives can mean sharing with them, gaining their support and educating them about alternative lifestyles, or it may mean being challenged and inappropriately judged about your adult-child's lifestyle or about your role as a parent. The following chapter is about how to talk with friends and relatives, and how relate to them in a way that is supportive to both you and your adult-child.

10.

Talking with Friends and Relatives

"How's your son doing?" your best friend asks innocently. "I hear that your daughter moved to California," your sister remarks, hoping you'll give her the inside scoop. "Your son's life sounds quite *interesting*," comments your boss one afternoon over coffee. Every family "crisis" brings with it the challenge of whom to talk with about what or how much to say about it. Whereas some parents are relatively unconcerned and indifferent about the way in which their friends and relatives respond to their adult-child's choice, other parents are very concerned with the reactions of others. Since there are numerous factors that contribute to both the degree of the parents' concern, as well as to how the information they share with their friends and relatives will be received, no clear-cut answers or easy formulas apply. Getting clear about our own thoughts and feelings will be our greatest asset in determining what to say to others.

Where Do You Stand?

Can you take an honest assessment of your degree of concern about the way in which your friends and relatives view your adult-child's lifestyle? Can you refrain from making any value judgements about what you discover? Generally speaking, some parents are terribly ashamed of their adult-child's lifestyle choice and very concerned about how others perceive them (the parents) as a result. Other parents are essentially proud of their adult-child's choice of lifestyle, and completely unconcerned with how other's view either them or their adult-child. Most of us probably fall somewhere in between these extremes on the spectrum.

Optimally, you will feel secure enough about your relationship to your adult-child and accepting of his or her choices to be relatively unconcerned about the way other people respond. This position is not only beneficial to your adult-child, but allows you to feel much lighter and happier when you are not bogged down by the weight of other peoples' opinions. Among the parents who fall into this category are both those who are genuinely proud, supportive and happy about their adult-child's choice of lifestyle, as well as those who may not agree with her choice, but who nonetheless recognize that their adult-child is her own person and that her choices are neither a positive nor a negative reflection on them.

Whether or not this parent agrees with his adult-child's lifestyle, he remains focused on the primary importance of supporting her and of maintaining a loving relationship with her. He feels a connection to her, but his identity is not wrapped up in the choices she makes. When choosing what to share with his friends and relatives, he tends to consider *who the person is* who wants to know, and how this person will receive what is shared rather than how that person will view him as a parent.

The mother of two adult-children who live in a spiritually-based, alternative community serves as a peer counselor for parents in similar situations. She shares her perspective on this issue:

"I think that if you're proud of your children that it shouldn't make a difference what other people think. To so many people it does, and although I hear their stories about their awkwardness and discomfort, and I understand what they are saying, I find it difficult to relate to. It seems the older I get, the less I care about what other people think. One time I read, 'Being self-conscious is useless because so many other people are busy being self-conscious that they don't even notice what you're doing.' I think that's right. I really don't care. If I accept a situation, I don't care

what society thinks. You've got to be willing to
ask yourself, 'How do I feel about the situation?' to trust your own sense of it, and to stand
behind that."

Unfortunately, as much as we would like to, many of us are
not able to feel this same ease about how our adult-child is perceived by our friends and relatives. As we discussed in Chapter 6:
Psychological Issues, parents commonly regard their adult-child
as an extension of themselves. They are so closely identified with
this false identification that they imagine other people are evaluating them based on their adult-child's lifestyle. This concern is
most prevalent among those parents who have difficulty in letting
go of their adult-child, i.e., allowing her to become an adult.
When a parent recognizes that his child is now a mature adult with
a mind and will of her own, he also understands that his adult-
child's choices are not primarily a reflection on him, but are instead an expression of who she is as an individual.

Parents who are involved in a particular social milieu or who
belong to certain political or religious groups also tend to be especially concerned with other's opinions about their adult-child's
lifestyle. These parents fear alienation from, or rejection by peers
and co-workers, or by the group to which they belong. This can
be a difficult situation. Some people *will be* shocked or scandal-
ized. Some people will reject these parents. There will come a
point in which parents will have to make some choices about how
much the approval of their peers and co-workers is worth to them
if it means having to further alienate their adult-child or lie about
his or her lifestyle. *The fact of one's adult-child choosing to live
an alternative lifestyle is nothing to be ashamed of.*

What To Tell — What Not To Tell

When deciding what to share about your son or daughter's
lifestyle with a given friend or relative, it is once again important

for you to remember that society as a whole tends to be misinformed, as well as closed-minded, about what it means to live an alternative lifestyle. Since widespread biases abound, failure to take this into account when speaking to others can be a set-up for misunderstanding. On the other hand, if you choose not to speak about your adult-child altogether, for a fear of being misunderstood by friends or relatives, you forfeit the opportunity to share with others your genuine questions, concerns, and interest in your adult-child's life, as well as the potential chance to widen their perspective about non-traditional lifestyles.

One factor for you to consider at this point is who your listener is. Are you speaking with someone who is genuinely willing to hear what you have to share, or with someone whose conversation tends to be superficial and for social purposes only? If you are speaking with someone who is not going to pay close attention and consideration to what you have to say, it is probably a good idea to err on the side of sharing very little information, as to do otherwise would be like "throwing pearls to swine."

You may wish to ask yourself: "What is my friend or relative's motivation for asking about my adult-child's lifestyle?" "Is this person earnestly interested in knowing about my adult-child, or is he asking in order to be polite or because he feels obliged to?" "Does this person have a strong bias about alternative lifestyles in such a way that he will use anything I say to validate his bias?" "Is it important for this person to understand my adult-child's lifestyle?" and, "Is there a way in which this person might benefit from learning about my adult-child's lifestyle and my relationship to her?"

While these questions are useful to heighten your sensitivity about what you communicate to your friend or relative, it is equally important that you not to be too certain about what you imagine another person's response will be. Not only will people surprise you at times, but if you are ashamed of your adult-child's lifestyle you may assume that others will feel the same way, whereas often they will not. Furthermore, as will be discussed in the following section, the way in which your friend or relative will respond to what you share depends not only upon his attitudes and disposition, but also upon the way in which you communicate with him.

After you have considered these questions, as well as the other considerations raised in this chapter, your choices about what to share and what not to share with friends and relatives will be largely a matter of trial and error. You may wish to start slowly — to share a small amount of information with a friend or relative and see how he or she responds to this before deciding to share more. Experience confirms that as time goes on you will acquire an ability to discern who to speak to and how much to share about your adult-child's lifestyle. Many parents still feel badly when they are unable to speak with certain close friends about their adult-child's life, or when specific relatives avoid this topic entirely. These parents have come to know and accept the limitations of other people's understanding. Yet they remain comfortable and solid with their own love for their adult-child. The mother of a popular spiritual teacher shares her perspective on this:

> "My close friends know exactly who my son is. When they ask me about him, I tell them, 'He has a group. He's a guru. He's a spiritual leader.' In other situations, I don't tell people a thing. People ask me what he does for a living and I say, 'He does all sorts of things. He runs a couple of businesses. He makes a living and enjoys where he lives,' and I leave it at that. I decide what to share according to the intelligence of the people. I wouldn't tell people who didn't know what I was talking about. If I meet people who are intelligent and interested, and they ask me what my son does, I tell them. I find out where a person stands, I tell them the truth when I want to, and I can lie whenever I feel I have to lie, when I feel like it's not their business."

Communication Skills

How you communicate is often as important as *what* you communicate. Your communication skill will largely depend upon your personal motivations, your ability to pay attention to and be flexible about the needs of the given situation, and your willingness to continuously engage in a process of discernment and intuition.

Your underlying motivation for sharing information with friends and relatives will come through in your communication to them, though it may be unspoken and even unconscious to you. If you share with your friend or relative because you feel good about your adult-child, and you feel that this person is genuinely interested in knowing about her, your communication will have an openness and clarity to it, and will likely arouse enthusiasm. If you are seeking approval for your adult-child's choices, your communication will carry with it a subtle tone of persuasion, and they are likely to respond with a certain authority about the issue; if you wish to seek consolation for the terrible choice your adult-child has made for the situation you are placed in, your communication will be dramatic and exaggerated, and they are likely to respond with concern and pity.

An unconscious dynamic frequently occurs when parents who are very anxious and concerned about their adult-child's lifestyle speak to others about this. If a parent believes that his adult-child is in a dangerous cult, he will "see" signs of this everywhere — even when it is not so. We see what we want to see, or rather, we see what our fear sees. Similarly, when speaking with friends and relatives, if a parent supports his fears with selected stories, and conveys his doubts with a certain degree of conviction, he will communicate these fears and doubts in a way that is completely convincing. Friends or relatives are likely to take on these fears for themselves, reflect them back in their alarm, and in doing so, provide further support for his worries and concerns. Everybody has probably had the experience of being completely, even if only temporarily, persuaded about something based on a convincing speech. We need to recognize this tendency so that we will not get caught in the trap of our own fears, believing we are genuinely communicating with another person when in fact we only seek validation of our own concerns.

Strive to be concise in your communication — by paying close and continual attention to the external situation as well as to your own emotional filters, you will gain greater clarity about what you intend to say. At the same time, maintain an openness to the constantly changing circumstances. Be flexible about what and how you choose to communicate depending upon who is present, the degree of the others' receptivity to what you are saying and your overall feeling about the situation. In other words, you will have to stay on your toes and be ready to alter the course of your communication in midstream when this is demanded. Your ability to accurately size-up the needs of the situation will call on your capacity for discernment and intuition. While everybody inherently has these abilities, they are strengthened only by giving them attention . . . experimenting with them.

As a parent, you may or may not have the capacity to change how you actually feel about your adult-child and her choice of lifestyle, but you do have the freedom to choose how you will convey this to others — if you will recreate your own reactions in your friend or relative in order to validate your feelings, or if you will accept your reactions and feelings for what they are, while communicating in a way that conveys a sense of honor and respect for your adult-child.

No matter how precisely and clearly you communicate about your adult-child's lifestyle, remember that people will have their judgements and opinions and there is little you can do about this. People who are close-minded and opinionated are unlikely to waver in their perspective. What you can do, however, is make a conscious effort to not take this personally, and to not take on their fears and judgements as if they were your own. Don't allow other people's reactions to influence your own inherent sense about your adult-child's well-being.

Deciding When Not To Tell

At times you will know that it is inappropriate to share information about your adult-child's lifestyle with certain people. This is markedly distinct from being ashamed. Instead, this choice is based on your knowledge that this person will not be able to really hear you, and is likely to have strong reactions or value judgements in response to what you say. In other words, you recognize that sharing this information has no value — to the person you are speaking to or to yourself.

When a parent is ashamed of his adult-child's lifestyle, he wants to hide this from others. He changes the conversation, alters the details or avoids speaking about it altogether with his friends and relatives. He fears their judgements, is embarrassed about the situation and considers it a secret. The parent who recognizes that it is inappropriate to talk about his adult-child's lifestyle in a particular situation may also change the subject, alter the details or avoid the matter altogether, but he does so from an entirely different context. He knows that to speak would be disrespectful and dishonoring to his adult-child, and upsetting to his friend or relative.

Try to avoid getting caught up in any rigid ideas about what it means to be honest with friends and relatives and so fail to recognize the needs of the moment and of the individuals involved. For example, many people will routinely ask about your adult-child's lifestyle when they are in fact not at all interested. Social convention for relatives and friends dictate that they ask one another about their children. In this case, you should feel no obligation to go into detail. When you can distinguish between another person's gesture and her genuine interest, you will know how to best respond .

Taking responsibility for being sensitive in our communication with others, while remaining steady in our love for our children, creates solid and clear relationships with others. *Every* family has skeletons in the closet that should neither be ignored nor used to frighten people. The knowledge gleaned from learning to be wise in communicating about your adult-child's choice of lifestyle will inevitably spill over into your relationship with your spouse, friends, relatives and other aspects of your life as well.

174

11.

Letting Go
and Looking Ahead

Congratulations . . . you've made it this far. Not that you have necessarily come to a place of deep resolve about your adult-child's lifestyle, or that you suddenly feel full and content — life may still seem quite tough. However, you have been willing to pick up this book, read it and consider the ideas presented within these pages, which is more than most parents are willing to do. For so many people, this situation is too scary and painful. They attempt to cope by pretending that it does not exist, or by seeking to remedy it with approaches that are driven by panic, instead of facing the fear and pain that lie at the root of it. Having come this far, you might even have discovered that, despite your pain, there is a tangible quality of satisfaction in being willing to meet a challenge eye to eye.

Do not be surprised, however, if issues you thought you had overcome resurface once again — this does not mean that your efforts have been in vain. Working through the stages described in this book occurs in a cyclical fashion, like a spiral that grows wider and deeper each time it circles itself. As these cycles continue you will experience each stage as deeper, more poignant and more fleeting. However, if you do not resist this natural progression, the cycles will quickly pass.

At this stage you stop fighting. You allow your adult-child to go on about her life in whatever form she chooses. You either agree, or you agree to disagree; you continue to feel frustrated by her choices, or you feel pleased for her happiness; you dwell in your loss, or you feel the pain and accept your present reality. The choices are really quite simple. You stay stuck or you move on.

There simply comes a time in his relationship with his adult-child when a parent must ask himself, "Do I love my daughter enough to want her to be free?"

Most parents, if they sincerely ask themselves this question, will find that they only wish for their adult-child's freedom despite the pain they may feel in allowing this. Deep within, they really don't want to control their adult-child's life. As a parent wishes to be free to make his or her own choices, including the so-called wrong ones, and to live according to his highest ideals, so he wishes this for others, especially his adult-child.

Letting Go

"At a certain point, a parent has to say to himself, 'I've done all I can do to raise my child and I have to let him go and trust that he will be O.K., and if he gets involved with the wrong people or the wrong organization, I have to trust that he will work through that as well. I've done my job in raising him and now it is my job to simply be there for him.'"

You do not let go of your relationship with your adult-child; instead, what you let go of is whatever keeps you from genuine relationship with him or her. Letting go is a form of freedom, a feeling of openness, an attitude of allowing. It is this overall sense of spaciousness and relaxation that is referred to when people say, "I feel like I've just had a hundred pound weight lifted off my back."

Letting go of your adult-child never implies that the underlying love between you diminishes in any way, or even that contact between you will become less frequent. In fact, often when you and your adult-child are able to release one another, the contact between you will actually become greater and the love more authentic. You are each free to express your love out of the fullness of your regard for one another, instead of from a weighted sense of obligation.

"Although they would probably never admit it, my parents seem to be much more pleased with me since I dedicated myself full time to spiritual study and community life. They're not pleased with what I'm doing, but our relationship is better. When I got involved in true spiritual life, I began to see the necessity of kindness, respect, and honoring my family in a way that I could not see when I was out protesting and rebelling. My parents thought that my choice to live in a spiritual community would bring a disruption to our relationship, but on the contrary, our relationship has really improved."

There will be sacrifices that a parent must make for the sake of his adult-child's freedom. In order to let go you may have to sacrifice your dreams for your adult-child, and your desire to shape her life. You will probably sacrifice the belief that she *belongs* to you and that you are ultimately responsible for her. You will sacrifice your fears about the consequences of her choice to pursue a different form of spirituality or lifestyle, and your belief that she is incapable of discerning for herself if she has made wise choices. You sacrifice the comfort of the old ways of relating to her in the service of new forms of connection that are now more appropriate. While many people can bring themselves to make certain physical sacrifices, one's beliefs, ideas and habits that have been used to maintain a sense of cohesiveness and control in relationship are often the hardest things to let go of.

However, there are no guarantees. In *letting go* there is freedom — to stay or to leave. When you "set your adult-child free," if he chooses to come back he does so of his own accord and because he has a genuine desire to be in relationship with you. He returns because his relationship with you nourishes him in some way — it adds a sense of wholeness and belonging in his life. If your adult-child does not return when you have set him free, he may be burdened with guilt, fearing he has betrayed you. (This attitude may lessen in time, especially if you continue to keep the door open.) Or, he may not return because he was never really "there" in the first place — what had been holding him to you may have been a sense of duty, or a physical or emotional dependency on you.

If you are willing to truly release your adult-child, rarely will he not return to you, for in being set free there is no longer anything he wishes to flee from. On the contrary, what awaits him in relationship to you is love, receptivity and acceptance.

The Paradox of Letting Go

Although you must let go of your adult-child completely and without the expectation of anything being reciprocated, when you do this with a sincere intention, you discover that often everything is returned to you . . . and more. This is the paradox of letting go. The principles which govern this exchange, however, cannot be bargained with. If your desire to release your adult-child is essentially motivated by what you anticipate in return, your letting go will lack sincerity and what gets returned to you may be minimal. However, when you release your adult-child for the sake of freedom (both his and yours!), that very freedom will grant you endless gifts — some of which you will see immediately in relationship with your adult-child, and others which will be felt as inexpressible qualities of joy, relaxation and wholeness within yourself.

> "It is as if you were holding a beautiful bird in your hand. When it was small, it needed you to feed and protect it, but it is grown now and can not live in the palm of your hand. You must release it."

When you let go of a relationship that is codependent and based on a feeling of insecurity, you may instead find yourself in a relationship that is founded on interest, care and genuine concern. When you let go of trying to mold your adult-child to be someone or something in particular, you will see that her own uniqueness begins to emerge, and you can in turn enjoy the expression of her essence, seeing her for what feels like the first time. When you are no longer trying to keep your adult-child bonded to you, you can rest in knowing that she is in relationship with you because this is her genuine desire. When you let go of false assumptions of how your relationship with her is "supposed to be," you are met with true relationship. In such moments of understanding, a window of possibility is opened. You sense the endless potential for the expansion of this understanding or communion, and anything less pales by comparison. These rare moments are real, revealing the love and tenderness that lies both within you and all others when you cease to hang on to fear.

> "I was frustrated by Mia's choice to live on an ashram. Yes, I essentially trusted her judgement, but this seemed to be a real stretch from anything I had raised her to do. I struggled a great deal over this, wondering if I had done something wrong, if I had a responsibility to rectify it, or even if I should share my opinion. With great effort, I decided to keep quiet and let her do her thing. It all changed when I received a birthday card from her — to this day it is among the most loving gestures she has ever shared with me. The letter said many things, but part of it went like this:
>
>> 'For everything you have given me, I am really grateful (and I'm not just saying that to have something mushy to say), and I'm going to do my best to give back what I've been given. Life can get really complicated, but right now I am depending on the simple things you taught me back when. They were things I could have only dreamt of being given . . . I wish I had words to express my

gratitude, but I hope you know it anyway. If not, I'll do my best to show you by really living from my heart, and listening to that small voice which tells me to keep going — that voice is the voice of my mom, along with the voice of my own heart now, which she taught me to listen to.'

I finally understood that she was living according to what I had taught her; it just looked different than I had imagined. I realized that there was no need to continue to feel guilty and in fact there was nothing to feel guilty for."

What is returned when you release your adult-child may also be completely unpredictable, seemingly unrelated, and nonlinear in nature — changes in your own life may begin to surface. For example, when you stop calling your adult-child every week to see if she is being fed well in her community, you may find that you are suddenly wearing your hair down and taking up dancing once again. Or, when you accept your son's choice to join a Catholic monastery, you may find yourself more playful and sensual in relation to your husband.

Keep in mind that once the process of release is in motion, you can either surrender to it or resist it. If you resist it, you will feel a great tension, as if you were trying to stop a boulder that was already rolling down a mountain. To the degree you are able, the best you can do is let the boulder go; cease any attempt at controlling its pace. In the same way you can allow your adult-child to be released. Trust in your heart that both you and she will be filled with something of greater value than what you have let go.

Thriving

> "Every seed destroys its container or else there
> would be no fruition."
> — Florida Scott Maxwell

Thriving occurs when you take the intangible riches you have gained by going through this process and turn your attention inward. This time, however, you no longer look within for the purpose of investigating your psychology or feeling your grief, but instead to expose the gold mine inside yourself.

There are riches hidden within everybody. The riches are not always shiny and apparent to the eye — not everybody is an undiscovered poet or a brilliant inventor — but there are qualities in each person that are exceptional and unique to that individual, and that can be used both to serve humanity and to bring joy to those around them.

Your gold mine may simply be your sensitivity to people and your ability to make others feel welcome. Your gold mine may be the joy and humor you can bring to a situation. Your gold mine may be your willingness to go out of your way to do things that are needed. Or, you may have hidden talents and abilities that you have been holding back or afraid to show.

Access to the gold within grows from our willingness to mine our grief. More than any other aspect of this process, it is your pain that reveals the depths where creativity and compassion live. You will not necessarily experience everything around you with clarity and tenderness, but you will find that there are subtle changes in the way you see the people and the situations in your life.

When you begin to thrive, you turn your focus back to your own life. Your attention is less centered on your adult-child (for you know she is doing what she wants to do), and is more focused on the people around you and the work or activities *you* are involved in.

It's About You Now

It's about *you* now! You return to yourself, perhaps with a bit of trepidation as you have not had so much time and space since your child was young, or perhaps you return to yourself for the first time. You find yourself faced with the questions, "What do I want now — for myself?" "What have I been thinking about doing for ages but have found reason after reason to postpone acting on?" Perhaps you want to focus your attention on your husband or wife, once again facing the challenge of deepening the intimacy between you, and on really enjoying one another's company. Maybe you want to finally plant the garden you have been talking about for years. Is now the time to finally begin a regular exercise program?

You may feel a desire to pursue personal interests — either re-engage old ones that you have neglected, or take up new hobbies or pursuits. By the time you are ready to consider your own life once again, you have let go of seeing your adult-child's lifestyle as a problem, and have recognized this whole experience as an opportunity for greater personal fulfillment. Mary, the mother of two adult-children who live in a spiritual community expressed:

> "I'm having too much fun being retired to worry about my children anymore. For years we worried and brooded over their choices. Where did that get us? Nowhere. Now my husband and I are traveling and doing what we want to do. Of course if they get sick we worry, but we're living our lives. We are confident that we raised our kids to be good people, and now we can move on. We're very fortunate to have our health and the resources to do what we want. You've got to let go and let your kids live their own lives — if they make mistakes, they make mistakes. Everybody does."

Thriving may also entail a decision to reach out to others beyond yourself and your immediate family. Rick, a long-term member of a popular self-help movement, describes how his parents learned to deal with the situation:

> "It was obvious after fifteen years that I wasn't about to change my mind about my involvement in this group, yet my parents complained ceaselessly. One day, I showed up at their house and told them I was going to take them out for the day. We proceeded to tour homeless shelters, old-age homes, residential treatment centers, slums, schools for the disabled, and orphanages. The whole day we visited people who really had something to complain about. My parents got it, and their lives changed. They weren't going to succeed in helping me because I didn't want help, but they got really involved in volunteer work and started helping the people who really needed help. I've never seen them so happy."

Rick's parents found an avenue in which to direct their pain. The pain of the people they were serving was much greater than their own personal pain, and in serving others, they transformed themselves. Service can be an excellent option for anyone who genuinely wishes to thrive.

Still Family

You are still family. Nothing will ever change that. The relationship that you now create with your adult-child is up to you. If you create a haven of love, acceptance, honor and a wide open heart within yourself, your adult-child will have a place there. In your heart you will have a relationship with him that will not be dependent upon how many times a year you see him . . . if he shaves his head . . . if he practices an unheard of religion or no religion at all . . . or if you are ever able to truly understand one another. The heart understands — you can trust that. The bond that exists between parents and children never dies — your children are alive in you, and you in them.

This book encourages parents to love their adult-children for who they are, and to allow them the freedom to become who they long to be. In the words of an old Jewish proverb:

> "There are two things parents can give their
> children — roots and wings."

Appendix
From Heartbreak to Healing:
Stories of Parents and Their Sons and
Daughters Who Have Been Through It

About the Stories

The people described in the stories related below are all in various stages of the process of working through the issues raised by their circumstances. Some are simply resigned; others express turbulent emotions; some have developed deep and loving relationships based on a genuine acceptance of one another. Names and certain details have been changed for purposes of confidentiality.

Clearly, many situations do not resolve themselves; some have very unfortunate endings. Often, either parents or adult-children feel too angry, hurt or threatened to be willing to even consider working toward restoring harmony in their relationship. The mass media, however, tends to thrive on examples of complete alienation and breakdown within families where an adult-child has chosen to live an alternative lifestyle. Such media attention leads the public to believe that *all* alternative lifestyles, communities and cults are destructive forces that result in the splitting-up of otherwise happy families. The following stories present another possibility.

While they don't all have "happily-ever-after" endings, these stories are about real people engaging real-life struggles who have come to recognize that they are still family, inextricably bonded to one another, and needing to eventually learn to adjust to their circumstances and to bring loving acceptance to one another.

Mary and Joe: "It's A Child's Prerogative to Choose His Own Lifestyle"

Through many years of struggle, and a clear intention to come to an understanding of their adult-children's choices, Mary, a sixty-four-year-old homemaker and community volunteer, and Joe, a sixty-seven-year-old retired telephone worker, have reconciled with the fact that their adult-children are living alternative lifestyles that are extremely different from what Mary and Joe had anticipated for them. The eldest of the three belonged to a widely criticized religious community, which he later chose to leave, whereas the other two, Jane and Tim, are long-term members of a small alternative community in the southwest that emphasizes Eastern spiritual values, including vegetarian diet, communal living and conscious childraising. Mary and Joe's story is a testimony not only to their acceptance of Jane and Tim's choices, but to their willingness to learn from them, and thereby enjoy some of the benefits of their lifestyle as well. Having come to understand the intricacies of the various cycles that parents go through when their adult-children choose to live alternative lifestyles, Mary and Joe now serve as peer counselors for other parents who are faced with these issues.

When Jane and Tim initially became involved in their present community, Mary and Joe were very worried. They had been through a great deal of turmoil with their first son, and feared that they were in for more of the same. Like all parents, they had no idea what the community was about, and feared that their adult-children were somehow in danger. According to Mary:

> "Initially, we were very concerned because once again what they were describing to us about their lives was so different than anything we had ever experienced. We asked them all kinds of questions about the community, always trying to remember to be sensitive and respectful to their responses. There were a lot of ups and downs in

that initial period. We visited them and stayed in
a hotel nearby for several days. We met their
friends, met the leader of the group and were
even invited to participate in a seminar that was
happening at the time. This all helped to ease
our concerns. It became obvious that there was
no imminent danger; there was no war. It was
just a different lifestyle — period."

Joe elaborated further:

"It's a terrifying thing for a parent, it really is.
You bring your kids up a certain way and all of a
sudden they're in an environment that is completely foreign to you and you hear all of these
stories about cults; you get all these ideas in your
mind . . . yet we always felt that our kids should
have a free choice to choose whatever lifestyle
they wanted. A parent needs to educate himself
about these things and speak to the child from a
place of genuine interest in his (the adult-child's)
life. There are some people who, even after they
do this, are going to continue to refuse to accept
their child. What a shame."

Due to their awareness of the need to allow their adult-children
to make their own life choices, instead of immediately reacting outwardly, Mary and Joe looked within themselves in an attempt to
understand their own turmoil. As Joe describes:

"This kind of thing makes a parent look deep
within himself. You've got to ask the questions
that you don't really want to know the answers
to. Most parents wanted to be something in their
lives that they never became — they had a secret

dream of becoming somebody big or important, and they keep a secret hope that their kids will attain the goals that they couldn't. They want to live their life through the kid and that's wrong. It suffocates the kid. If you have real definite ideas about what your child should do or be, it's going to be very, very difficult for you."

Both Mary and Joe largely attribute their ability to maintain bonded, loving relationships with their adult-child to their ability to have an open mind, and to the fact that they were not insistent that their adult-children adhere to any particular religion or belief system. Mary elaborated:

"The main concern that parents have when their adult-child chooses another lifestyle," explains Mary, "is the difference in belief systems. That's because most people have a concrete, specific belief system and anything that veers even slightly from that system immediately becomes wrong and bad no matter what it is. People should be able to believe whatever they want to. It is in no way necessary for parents and children to have the same beliefs in order to be in relationship with each other. For us it was not a matter of belief, we never tried to get them to believe anything. Our only concern was that what they were doing might present some kind of physical danger to them, and it quickly became obvious that this was not the case."

When parents recognize the inherent right of their adult-children to choose to believe as they wish, the struggles resulting from conflicting belief systems dissipate and no longer have the power to alienate them from one another.

Agreeing to disagree, and the willingness to accept their adult-children's lifestyle choices in spite of the fact that there are aspects of their lives that they do not understand, is a further element that has allowed Mary and Joe to maintain an ongoing supportive relationship with their adult-children. Joe commented:

> "There are some things I don't understand, and even that I don't agree with, but I see the end results. I see them growing. Tim has learned to sing and act, in addition to becoming an excellent businessman, and Jane has excelled in music and the children there love her. I see them doing things they would normally never do, and I see them just as loving — maybe even a little bit more loving toward us — as they have ever been."

Mary believes that when a parent makes a clear decision to *agree to disagree* with her adult-child, that this has the power to mend any rift in the relationship between them.

> "It's only in their belief system that they've changed, and that's their choice to make. I don't go along with it. I don't believe what they believe and I wouldn't take it on for myself. It would not be what I would choose, but that's my own choosing. I've got my own beliefs. It is a child's prerogative to choose his own lifestyle. My children and I essentially agree to disagree."

Mary and Joe have come to value the importance of maintaining clear communications and ongoing contact with their adult-children. After extensive struggles in learning to communicate with their eldest son about his lifestyle and religious beliefs, they arrived at the recognition that a parent's ability to communicate with discernment and clarity is one of the most essential elements in maintaining strong and loving ties with his or her adult-child. Mary remarked:

> "We initially didn't realize that what you don't say is just as important as what you do say and how you say it. You don't just say everything on your mind. You can still talk with them freely, but when you're going to comment on their lifestyle, you think before you talk."

Joe added further:

> "If you love your kids, you've got to stay in contact with them and learn about them no matter what. Maybe you won't like what you learn, but you've got to learn. The more you know about any subject on this earth, the better off you are."

Although Mary and Joe were open-minded concerning their adult-children's choices from the beginning, there was a gradual process by which they came to deeply accept and respect their lifestyles. Mary explained:

> "Acceptance is not easy. It's like when somebody makes the decision to give up smoking. It just doesn't happen over night — it takes work. It comes with time, patience and a real interest in them as people."

Joe extrapolated further:

> "We've had to struggle through it and it's been rough at times. It's only through maintaining communication with the kids, trusting them, keep-

ing an open mind and I guess most importantly, seeing the results, that you come to a kind of peace about it. But looking back, it's taken some time. Every year we feel better about it. The main thing I've learned over the years is that Jane and Tim are essentially still Jane and Tim. There are changes in them, but they are positive ones. Our love is definitely stronger for having gone through this together."

As with many parents who have utilized the opportunity of their adult-child's choice for self-reflection and to deepen their relationships with them, Mary and Joe have seen the benefits that can result from this situation — both in relationship with their adult-children, and also for their adult-children themselves. Mary commented:

"You learn things you never thought you'd know about. You think about things you had never considered. We always told them, 'Be good, don't break the law, don't hurt anybody and be happy.' They've done just that. We have many, many friends who know our kids and think they're wonderful. We do too. We were able to accept and understand them. In a way we have an even closer relationship with them now — we've had to talk about things more openly and get into the nitty-gritty with one another. That can build relationship. There are still things we don't agree with, but that's not our prerogative to even worry about."

Joe elaborated further on the benefits that he has seen in both Jane and Tim:

> "I think that in a lot of ways Jane and Tim's involvement in their group has made them develop a broader sense of communication with other people and brought them out even more in their way of thinking about others. They're very compassionate, very loving and very caring people — both to us and to others — which means an awful lot in this world today."

Having come to a clear understanding of what parents go through when their adult-children choose to live alternative lifestyles, Mary and Joe have since counseled many parents who are dealing with similar issues, though the circumstances may vary. Through this counseling work, Mary and Joe have come to recognize the common sources of tension and the places where parents and their adult-children persistently get stuck in their relationships with one another.

They have discovered that the most frequent source of alienation among families results from a parent's concerns and reactions when her adult-child chooses to pursue a spiritual or religious life that is different from that of her parents. Mary described:

> "A lot of people call me and are very upset because their child or loved one is attending a different church than the one the parents go to, or because their child is a vegetarian and is praying in another language. I ask them, 'Why are you concerned about them?' They tell me it's because they're child is not going to be saved, or that they're going to go to hell, or that now they believe 'such-and-such' or 'so-and-so.' They're not really concerned that anything bad is hap-

pening to their child physically or mentally, or
that he's being abused in any way, it's just that
he's taken on a different way of thinking than
what his parents have brought him up to think —
to me that's wrong. When they can't reconcile
with this, the parents will sometimes turn their
backs on their children and completely disown
them, which is too bad because there are many
other ways to be that would result in a happier
ending."

Joe remarked:

"Some people say my wife and I are very spiritual. I guess we don't completely understand the
term. We love and accept our children unconditionally — maybe that's what they mean by spiritual. We're not religious, and this may have
helped us in accepting our children because we
raised them to be whatever they wanted to be —
and believe me, they turned out to be just that!
But some parents raise their kids in a certain religion and if they seek out another religion which
is kind of 'far out' they can't see beyond that."

Mary and Joe have come to see that when parents argue with
their adult-children about their choice of lifestyle, this will frequently result in the adult-child feeling insulted and hurt, if not altogether alienated. Mary reiterated:

"I tell them not to argue. You can't imagine how
many heartbreaking stories I've heard — parents who never got along with their children in
the first place will argue with them about their
church or their financial situation. They'll insult

them and alienate them, and then say that the child's group has convinced him that his parents don't care about him and that he shouldn't have contact with them. If all their parents do is fight with them, why would the children call?"

Mary continually stresses the need for parents to look within themselves in order to recognize what their priorities are in relationship with their adult-children:

"Parents have got to examine their own feelings and decide what kind of relationship they want to have with their children, because nobody wants to be bullied and pushed and argued with all the time about any belief — whether someone converts to Catholicism, Judaism or Hinduism. A parent needs to be very caring, loving and understanding. That's about all they can do unless they want to be belligerent and lose contact with their children altogether and that would be devastating."

There is a fundamental shift that occurs when parents are able to accept their adult-children and their choices. Mary summarized:

"People who do accept their child's lifestyle no matter what it is, even if they never understand it, continue to have a relationship with their children. Parents have got to be willing to really listen to their children, because relationships that are superficial and constantly strained are not really relationships at all. For the most part, parents seem to bring this upon themselves. You can agree to disagree with anybody, but most parents aren't willing to do this with their children, they want to mold them. We didn't agree with our oldest son's choice, and initially we didn't agree with Jane and Tim's choice either, but it's not our life. It's not up to us to tell them what to do in any situation. In one way, children will always be children to their parents no matter what age they are, but it is also true that they are mature adults. Most parents can't accept that their children are grown adults."

Joe concluded:

"Most importantly, it's never too late to start. Beneath all superficial differences, parents and their children share a fundamental wish to have a loving relationship with one another."

Walter and Anne: "We All Hear Her Cry, 'Who Am I?'"

The following story describes the process of growth and learning that Walter, a government worker, and his wife Anne, a homemaker and nurse, went through when their daughter Francesca ran away in order to live on an alternative "hippy" commune. This story is distinct from the other accounts of adult-children shared throughout the text in that Francesca is a young teenager, and the choices she made were not necessarily adult choices. However, irrespective of the "rightness" or "wrongness" of her choices, Walter and Anne understood the need to keep an open door to their child despite her behavior toward them or the lifestyle she chose to lead. Furthermore, they were faced with the painful recognition that the way they parented Francesca had strongly influenced the choices that she would later come to make. Walter and Anne are examples of parents who were willing to get help for themselves instead of blaming their child, while at the same time not becoming disabled by paralyzing guilt.

Walter began:

"Francesca thought that eating blue-green algae and eating wheatgrass would keep her from getting AIDS. That's what they told her at the hippy gatherings she would attend. She was only thirteen years old.

From the time she was ten years old, she was isolating from her friends at school. At age eleven she was associating with gangs and using drugs. She was skipping school and engaging in sexually promiscuous activities. She was kicked out of summer camp that year, threatening suicide when we wanted to send her to Catholic school.

When she was fourteen, Francesca ran away from home for the second time. This time, she didn't return for many months. She had been on Prozac™ (an anti-depressant) for six weeks, and we had recently attended a family therapy session during which we all 'dumped on her.'

When she left home this time, she hitchhiked all around the country. She was living in the back of a U-Haul with twenty people and had lice. She jumped off a truck. She was caught shoplifting for cigarettes. She was going to go to Mexico for the winter. She ended up 'settling down' in a traveling hippy commune.

She was running to save her life. I understand her because of what I went through in my teenage years. Instead of killing herself, she went on the run. From what? From those dark and painful feelings that plague so many teenagers. She said that she felt like if she stayed anywhere for more than a week that she'd go crazy. She was afraid of her feelings and so were we. In her runaway note, she said she was going on a spiritual quest. My wife and I are agnostics, and Francesca felt that she needed a spirituality of some kind. She was looking for some kind of peace.

I have a soft spot in my heart for Francesca's group. They believe in magic and all that kind of stuff, but they are a gentle group. They all told her that she'd be better off at home with a loving family, but when she refused, they agreed to take care of her. We figured she was better off there than on the streets where she'd be forced to take to prostitution."

In a piece of writing she sent her parents, Francesca shared the following:

> "I put up a wall between me and my family. I hated myself and everyone around me . . . In ninth grade I decided that I didn't have enough freedom to do my drugs and I didn't think that I could live with my parents whom I thought were out to get me. They were my parents and that made them the enemy . . . I never cared that I was hurting them . . . I just didn't care. I didn't care about my family because I didn't care about myself."

Francesca's mother Anne "shut-down" in the midst of the crises. Numbing themselves, or becoming indifferent, is one way that people attempt to deal with painful feelings:

> "It's hard for me to get in touch with my feelings. I tend to stay very logical and rational and be ready for any decisions that need to be made — I do it as a means to get by from day to day. It helps me to stay distanced and detached from it just so that I can function and not get all tied up in it."

Walter, on the other hand, had stronger emotional reactions:

> "I'd go from crying my eyes out to feeling absolutely helpless. We were very tired; we were just so tired of fighting with her. We were very afraid, but what could we do?"

Irrespective of their distinct reactions, Walter and Anne both recognized the fact that Francesca's choice to run away and pursue and an alternative lifestyle was not only Francesca's "problem," but was a result of how they had parented her, as well as a reflection upon what was going on in their relationship with each other. It is a common principle in family psychology that children often act out the unexpressed tension and problems in their parent's relationship. Anne described:

> "I suffer from depression. I wrote a letter to Francesca last night talking about how we pass on this kind of mess from mother to child. My mother was depressed when I was a baby, and I think that's why I had trouble when Francesca was a baby. These kind of depressive undertones tend to color everything in one's life. However, I didn't understand these things then. If I had been in touch with my feelings then and worked through these issues, I don't think Francesca would have had to run away. Beyond this, my relationship with Walter had begun to deteriorate, and this must have been affecting her."

Walter added:

> "We're making some changes. It's been rough on us. This kind of situation really reveals what's beneath the surface. My wife and I have almost broken up. I hope it will work out — we just don't know."

Sometimes parents feel valid remorse. When they recognize that they have made errors in raising their children, grief is likely to be present. However, when feelings of remorse turn into paralyzing guilt, the value of the pain is lost — for grief is an organic

202 When Sons and Daughters Choose Alternative Lifestyles

process of life, while guilt is an avoidance of true feeling. In Anne's words:

> "A parent has to stop kicking herself at some point. Eventually, parents have to start to live their lives to their satisfaction, and if their child is off doing crazy things, they have to allow him or her to take responsibility for it. I can talk about the things I did wrong, and the things I didn't do, but although I will do everything I can for Francesca, I have to allow her to get over the disadvantages of her childhood, and perhaps even use them to develop character traits.
>
> I can't help but to feel some guilt. Most parents know logically, though few admit it, that a lot of this comes from the home. Where else can it come from? Deep inside, we know this and we wish things would have been different."

Walter and Anne have been able to come through this to the degree that they have because of their willingness to get help. Walter explained:

> "I've had support. My boss at work has been very supportive. She's got a sister who's in a similar predicament. We've also been in family therapy. You need to talk to people about these things . . . Parents should get into some form of therapy, and not necessarily for their kid, but for themselves."

Throughout the process of healing and reconciliation, Walter and Anne were very honest in their relationship with Francesca. Walter described:

"Right after she left home, we called up her commune and asked them to tell her that we loved her. We wrote to her all the time. We told her we were in therapy and that we wanted her to come home. She knew that the police had called us when she was caught shoplifting. We wanted her to know that we loved her no matter what she did or who she was with."

In this way, Francesca's parents conveyed to her that there was always an open door should she decide to return home. In the case of a teenager, it is essential that parents communicate clearly to their child that she is welcome back to their home whenever she wishes, and that she will neither be blamed nor shamed for her leaving in any way. However, in order to keep the door open on a deeper level, parents must learn what it is that will allow them to keep their hearts open, and to work through any blocks that may impede this from happening. According to Walter:

"Parents need to know their bottom line. What will you do to save your kid? Will you change yourself? Will you change your lifestyle? Will you change the way you view the world? You have to know who you are. Your child needs you to be a rock — that doesn't mean that you should be hard — it means that you know what your values are.

You have to be able to say to yourself, 'I believe my child can be successful in life.' You have to believe she can make it — otherwise, what's the point? You're not believing in her."

The story of Francesca's reconciliation with her parents is not yet complete. After being picked up by the police as a runaway, she agreed to go to a residential treatment home for teenagers where she will stay until her physical, emotional and mental health returns. What remains clear, however, is that her parents are committed to their relationship with their daughter, in spite of the mutual hurt that has occurred between them. Walter concluded:

> "Our goal, is to stay together as a family. Yet we can't force her to come home — that wouldn't be right. As for Francesca, I want her to know herself. She has qualities in her that I really admire, but she has to be alive and clear within herself in order to use them. I want her to be able to make decisions that will allow her to have many options in the future. I wish only the best for her — the way that will look is anybody's guess."

Chandra: "I Couldn't Help but to Love Them — They Were My Parents"

Chandra, a forty-four-year-old concert pianist from Germany, reconciled her relationship with her parents throughout a twenty year struggle which ensued when she began to live an alternative lifestyle. This account testifies to the extremes to which some parents will go to as a result of their fear and lack of understanding of their adult-child's lifestyle, including how they will treat their adult-children as incapable of making mature decisions. It illustrates that harmony can be sustained within families, even amidst immense adversity, by holding on to the common ground of love that underlies relationships. Although the struggle within Chandra's family endured for many years, reconciliation need not take this long. It is possible to learn from the failures and shortcomings of others.

At the age of twenty-four, Chandra went to live in a small community that practiced organic farming in southern Germany. She left that community six years later, and by the time she was thirty, Chandra was married and living in the same city as her parents. She and her husband then began to follow a set of principles set forth by an intentional community in England to which her sister belonged. This group advocated a macrobiotic diet, specific Yogic exercises and homeopathic health care.

"I learned from a very young age that as long as I did what my parents wanted me to do things were fine, but if I strayed even a little bit off track from where they wanted me to be, there would be hell to pay.

I knew my parents wouldn't like what I was up to in terms of my affiliation with the community, even though I was leading a perfectly normal life in terms of living in a house, driving a car, and having good friends and lucrative work, so I decided to hide my interests from them in an effort to not disturb them unnecessarily. However, my mother began to snoop around my house and discovered books and letters and vitamin supplements that she was unfamiliar with. Without talking things over with us, she concluded for herself that my husband and I were engaged in cultic activities.

Things got really bad after that. My mother and father would try to physically restrain me from leaving when I would visit their home. They'd use every available chance to tell me that I was ruining my life and throwing away all my opportunities. One time I began to walk out when the yelling became too much and my father pin-ned me down on the kitchen floor and held me there — I was thirty years old!

I was in a terribly distraught state for years. I couldn't eat because I was so upset — I turned to skin and bones. I was so excited about what I was doing in one domain, but my parents just wouldn't let up harassing us. They would show up at our house whenever they wanted. My father actually punched my husband in the face and broke his nose when he said something he didn't like about vegetarianism. There was general hatred, violence and persecution in my family, and it reached the point where I had to call the police when they came over. They were not willing to listen to anything I had to say about what I was doing — not one single idea. They had already decided that I was in a cult and that I was going down. They were treating me like an infant who had no mind of her own — no intelligence, nothing, and I had been living on my own for years.

When my mother began to investigate the idea of cults and brainwashing and all of that kind of thing, she found the perfect ammunition to rationalize all of her actions and prove her point of view. She'd say, 'Chandra's not in her right mind because she is brainwashed.' All that the cult material did was to give her justification for her perspective and make it literally impossible to talk to her about my lifestyle until this day. She takes anything I say about my life and twists it in order to support her ideas about me. For example, she can see that I am radiantly happy. She can see that I'm healthy. She can see that I enjoy what I'm doing and that I have a lot of friends. But instead she'll say things like, 'You seem so young and vibrant and lighthearted, they sure keep you from growing up there, don't they?' Or, 'You've become so educated in the field of spirituality — I guess you have a lot of time to read when you can't go out.' "

When Chandra was thirty-seven, the issue intensified still further:

"I got a phone call from my sister who was living on the farm in England. (My parents had her and her husband kidnapped and put them through a six week deprogramming, when she was seven months pregnant.)

I did not want to be kidnapped and deprogrammed, so I decided to disappear. I told my parents, 'We are going to disappear because you will not leave us alone. I'll give you an address where you can write to, but it will not be the address of where I'm living. I'm not going to cut you off 100%, but I'm not going to see you anymore.' I didn't want to do it, but I had no other choice.

None of this meant that I didn't love my parents. I still love my parents. The issue was one of dignity and integrity — both mine and theirs. There are groups that tell people that they shouldn't have anything to do with their parents, but I've never felt this way. My mother used to say that I cut her off because of the cult, but it was her own doing — she forced me to distance myself from her during those periods.

My husband and I started spending more time in England near my sister, who had returned to the community in spite of the deprogramming, and during one of these periods the government officials arrived to arrest us and tell us that we were illegal. Actually, this wasn't true, but my mother had called the consulate to say that we were in England illegally and had hired detectives to find us — she figured that the only way she could get me out of this so-called 'cult' was to have me evicted from the country. Four years and thousands of dollars in lawsuits later, we eventually got a resident's visa to stay in England."

Chandra was not willing to give up on her family bonds in spite of all of this. Eventually, she came to a turning point. She realized that she was going to have to make peace with her parents on some level — both for her own sanity and theirs.

"All of the difficulties we went through is like having been through a war; if you've been through a terrible war in which violent crimes have been committed, in this case emotional ones, you come out of it either a very embittered, miserable, sour, hateful person, or you gain a depth of understanding that allows you to have mercy for everyone involved in the circumstance, and to carry on from there with forgiveness and compassion for the human condition that makes us do such things to one another. I didn't want to be a miserable and unhappy person, so I decided that when old feelings of hatred and anger would come up, I would think to myself, 'We've just been in a war together. What can I do now to keep the peace?' There's a big lesson in this for everybody involved: Can you love people in spite of having seen them at their worst?"

Just as Chandra has essentially taught herself that she could bring compassion to an otherwise difficult situation, she similarly encourages parents to take responsibility for their own happiness.

"For parents who are depressed, unhappy, and who don't enjoy life, their child's lifestyle can become an excuse for their unhappiness. I have found that when my parents enter a period of depression or dissatisfaction in their lives, or when there are problems in their relationship, they immediately blame this on the fact that I have chosen a different lifestyle. I am not responsible for their unhappiness. My brother is fulfilling every one of their dreams but that hasn't made them happy. It's not an easy thing, but parents can feel the pain of their child's choices and still move on."

In an effort to create peace within her family, Chandra set up certain limits about what she was willing to talk about with her parents, and what she wasn't.

"I said to them, 'In order to maintain a loving relationship with you, I need to create some boundaries. I will not talk to you about what I'm doing, and if you bring up the subject and harass me about it I will leave.' I think it's O.K. to not have to talk about problems if there's no resolution possible. If you try talking and it looks like there's no possible resolve, why carry on talking? I already loved my parents, what I wanted now was relationship.

I told them that I didn't want to have the same argument every time we spoke to one another year after year after year. It was becoming too deadening. So I made an agreement with them. I said, 'Look, if you have a radical change of perspective about this issue, I want to hear about it immediately, and I will agree to do the same for you. If I have any sudden realization about this that is different from what you've heard from me already, I will inform you.' This agreement helped to keep each of us from thinking that we had to continually bring up the issue in order to ensure that any change in either of our perspectives would be communicated to one another. As far as I'm concerned, it is a law of human relationships that you don't give help unless it is asked for."

With clearer boundaries, the relationship between Chandra and her family began to improve.

"The reason we manage to have a pretty decent relationship, is that I finally managed to get through to my mother that it is O.K. to agree to disagree. There was a mutual recognition that

we could still be friends even though we have
very, very different views about most things."

   Making a conscious choice to relate to one another on common ground — to sustain their relationship based on commonality
instead of difference, is often one of the most important decisions
that parents and their adult-children can make in terms of sustaining harmony in their relationship with one another. Chandra explains it this way:

   "When my parents treat me like another human
   being leading an ordinary human life that is essentially no different from theirs, we can relate
   with one another on a human-to-human level.
   When they approach me from the perspective of
   saving me from something I don't want to be
   saved from, there's no way to relate except to
   push them away. What I've found with some
   people who have been anxious about my life but
   who have been willing to talk to me, is that if
   they let me relate my life to something in their
   experience — if we can find some point where
   we have common ground — the particular details
   of the way I go about my life are no longer
   threatening to them.
   I enjoy my parents, and there are still things
   that we share in common. I enjoy their enjoyment of life, because they are really able to enjoy
   good company, good food, good music and the
   outdoors. I can relate to them on that level. I
   think that if parents look to where they can enjoy
   their children, and if they allow their children to
   enjoy them where they are able to, this provides
   the foundation for a solid and strong relationship.
   Perhaps the key to sustaining relationships
   with those who are leading lifestyles that they

don't understand, is to relate from the heart.
When people relate from the heart, they say
things like, 'I don't know what you're doing and
if I thought about it I'd probably get upset about
it, but I'm looking at you and I see how you are
and I see that you're still someone I know.'
When people relate from feeling, they don't have
a problem with it. It is when they get stuck in
their heads and ideologies and such that it becomes difficult."

As so many parents and adult-children who have maintained
healthy relationships with one another have come to understand,
Chandra emphasizes the need for mutual respect.

"Respect is the main thing. You've got to respect people's choices, and the fact that they are
human beings with dignity. We learn from our
mistakes and sometimes we need to make big
mistakes in order to learn about certain things.
So, even if your child is making what appears to
be a serious mistake and you are not able to hon-
or her decision, treat her with respect. You've
got to trust enough in your parenting that even if
your child goes off and does some wild and crazy thing, if you did a reasonable job parenting
and instilled good values, those values are going
to come through in the long run. I feel as though
I am precisely living out the details that my parents taught me, it just doesn't look the way they
imagined it."

Chandra and her parents have learned from the mistakes they
have made and the shared pain that they have endured together.
She now sees them once a year and they frequently converse on

the telephone. When they do spend time together, they focus on shared interests and enjoyment of food, music and talk of old friends. From time to time, the same old issues resurface once again, but beneath the surface arguments, both Chandra and her parents know that Chandra will not change her mind about her life-style after twenty years, and what remains of value between them is the love they share. She concluded:

> "I grant my parents this — in spite of their anger, frustration and their trying to enforce their ideals on me, they have never withdrawn their love and their support for me as a human being. I still feel their love for me even if they express it in seemingly strange ways, and I still feel that they have a lot of regard for me as a human being. I understand that they're doing this because they really worry about me and that they think they're being helpful.
>
> You have to keep loving through all of it, even though you might not feel as though you do at different points. It's hard for parents and adult-children to maintain a relationship in the midst of such extreme differences and I'd say it is only the strength of love in my family, and the genuine desire for relationship that has allowed us this."

Julianne — "It's a Battle Between My Heart and Mind"

"In my heart I accept it and in my mind I am angry. I've always been a believer in destiny, faith, God — that's my belief system. I'm a very spiritual person, but I'm also very emotional. I have this battle going on because my soul knows that everything is as it should be, but then my emotions kick in and say, 'That's my baby.' When I'm really quiet and I contemplate the situation, I feel happy for her."

Thus began Julianne, a forty-five-year-old divorced mother of three children. Her story illustrates the way in which one woman is able to use her inherent spiritual understanding and faith to work her way through the grief she feels as a result of her daughter's choice to move away from home in order to live in a Buddhist community. It is also an example of how, through a willingness to acknowledge her own grief, a parent ceases to blame her adult-child for her pain, and instead opens herself up to the lessons of letting go and moving on.

Like most parents, in the beginning Julianne was shocked. She explained:

"The word 'commune' brings up a lot of pictures in peoples' minds. When Amy first told me she was moving away to live in a community, my stomach just flipped over. I went into a state of total denial — I carried on as if nothing was happening, always thinking, 'She might change her mind.' As time went on, however, I saw that this was a young woman who had clearly made up her mind — that was difficult to face. I have a really hard time with her being so far away. I don't know exactly what she's doing."

Julianne admitted that although she has a great deal of trust in Amy's intelligence, societal stereotypes and the opinions of others continually threaten to take her away from her own clarity about the issue.

> "My husband is a government worker. For him this is a nightmare. Everytime there is a newspaper article about cults or hippies, he rants and raves. When she first left, he said to me, 'Why don't you just tell her she can't go?' I looked at him and said, 'Roger, you can't tell a twenty-four-year-old what to do.
>
> It's not that the newspaper articles and publicity don't scare me too — they do. I also know that there are wonderful leaders out there who get too much power and the groups go sour. But you worry about your kids no matter what they do. You worry that when they drive to work that a drunk will hit them or something else will happen. I have to believe that Amy is a strong person — that she's mature and responsible. You can't really criticize what your kids are doing without subtly attacking their intelligence."

Having been raised in a strong Catholic environment, Julianne further struggled with how to deal with her family's responses to Amy's choices. She explained:

> "I was raised in an extreme religion. I have a lot of relatives who are ministers in the church. Every time I tried to talk to them about what Amy was doing, before I could get two words out of my mouth, they'd be challenging me and criticizing her choices. One year on Christmas eve, when they were questioning me yet again, I just

flipped . . . I never flip. I'm the silent structure in the family, but this time I had something to say. I told them that if we had stayed in the church, that Amy would be a missionary in Africa or India. I told them that this was so obviously her calling. I let them see how she is really out there doing service — she's a missionary, just not with a cross around her neck . . . They got that. They all know Amy, and when they really thought about it, they could see what I was saying; so they backed off.

If you're going to talk about your childrens' lifestyles at all, you've got to explain it in a language that people can understand. For people who are a part of the church, you've got to say things like, 'They've become disciples. They've heard their calling.' The disciples picked up and left because there was a call to serve. These children are following the call of God in the way that they hear it. Many people, when they think about it, can see the bigger picture — you call their attention to that. You try to educate people — some just won't get it."

Regardless of her trust in Amy, Julianne grieves the loss of her "child" as she watches her become a woman.

"There's a certain bond between mother and child. I have always been so proud to go places and be with my kids. I think everybody wants to do something really wonderful with their lives and I look at my kids and say to myself, 'I did that.' I grew up without a close family and I wanted to give my kids what I didn't have. I see them becoming strong because of what I have taught them. Now I have to be strong too.

Still, I miss her so much. I have pictures of her all around and I look at them and talk with my other children about her. My sustaining force now is knowing that she is happy. When she was growing up, she seemed very lost because she couldn't relate to people. Now she's met people who she admires and who respect her . . . It's a lot easier to cope knowing that she is happy. I have to be O.K. with it. If I fight and resist it, I know she'll shut me out.

I guess my main fear is that I've lost my daughter. 'Is she going to become so involved in her group that it becomes her whole life?' 'Will she ever get married and have a family and experience all of life?' 'Is she just going to move farther and farther away?' There's a part of me that hopes she'll just do what she needs to do there and come back; but really I know that's not the point. All the things you raise your kids to be, if they really learn them, take them away from you. I could have raised them to be really fearful and then they'd be attached to me — that's how I was raised. But if you raise your children to be free spirits, then you have to watch them do just that."

All loss brings grief with it. Grief does not signal a problem, but rather indicates the ongoing cycles of loss and growth as one moves through life. It is Julianne's ability to open to her feelings and to a deeper understanding that has given her the ability to cope with her situation so well, ceasing to blame Amy for her pain.

"I know that Amy is doing what she has to do. We're all here to do what we have to, and our only real choice is to fulfill that. Meanwhile, there's a great deal of growth in it for me. We gain our wisdom through situations like this — the more we can draw on our own strength or the strength of our faith, the better we learn to deal to move effectively through life.

This type of growth is like working on a muscle — you just keep at it even though it can be uncomfortable . . . I have to learn from the emotions instead of wallowing in them. You can't take short-cuts. You have to go through every little painful piece of it to get where you need to go. I'll only find out if I've made it when I get there! Underneath it all, however, I know I'm O.K. and that I'm doing what I have to."

It's been three years since Amy first joined the community. Since that time, Julianne's two sons have moved out of the home as well, and Julianne now finds herself at a new juncture, unsure which way she will go. Nonetheless, she is optimistic. She concluded:

"My children don't need me to be there anymore. My whole identity has been that I'm a mom. It's been my joy, but it's time to move onto something else. If they don't get married and have kids, I guess I'll never get to experience what it's like to become a grandmom. In my mind, I say to them, 'None of you are ever going to give me grandchildren?' (she laughs) . . . It's life and you just deal with it. You have to be adaptable to life.

I did the growing up thing. I did the mother thing. I've even been through menopause. Now I'm saying, 'What next?' Even though it was stressful, raising my kids was my peace and my joy. Now I must find something that will give me that for the next stage of my life. I'm looking for that . . . When I look in my heart, I know it's all right."

Charlotte — "How Does a Jewish Woman Have a Son Who's a Guru?"

Many people imagine the leaders of alternative movements and religions to be charismatic, overbearing and outspoken individuals who, in their own realm stand alone. Yet few take the time to consider the fact that they are ordinary people with parents and families just like anybody else. Charlotte is a widowed Jewish woman and the mother of a spiritual teacher, or *guru*, who has been presiding over a thriving spiritual community for the past twenty years. Irrespective of both the praises she continually hears from his students, and the stereotypes and biases she receives from the society-at-large, she has maintained a close and supportive relationship with her son throughout this time as she has watched both him and his community grow and mature over the years.

Although her son went from a traditional career in business to a full-time spiritual life, Charlotte knew from the beginning of this transition that in spite of any wishes she might have for him, she would need to allow her son to pursue the life he desired, whatever it might be.

"You know, every Jewish mother wants to have her son become a doctor — at least a lawyer if not a doctor — so when your son decides to do something different, you're a little surprised. None- theless, I couldn't tell him, 'Don't do this. Why don't you continue with your business which you were so successful with and were making money at?' I don't think he would have listened, and he would have been right not to. It has been clear all along that he is a grown man and should do just as he wants to. This is what he wants to do and that's just fine."

She attributes her ability to embrace her son and his lifestyle largely to her capacity to have an open mind. She explained:

> "My husband and I were open-minded people to begin with. We never said to him, 'This is what you should do, this is what you should not do.' We didn't have a closed mind . . . Since I was a child, I learned not to be a bigot but to accept other people's ideas. You don't have to join them, you just shouldn't criticize them for it."

Although she does not strictly adhere to the customs of her own religion, she has gained a respect for the wholeheartedness with which her son and the people in his community pursue their spiritual practices:

> "I've always admired people who have a strong religion no matter what it is. It doesn't matter what religion you follow as long as you really and truly believe in it. I envy those people."

Through her own experience, and as a result of meeting numerous parents of the members of her son's community, Charlotte has become acquainted with the difficulties that many parents have in accepting their adult-child's lifestyle. She explained:

> "Most parents think that this situation is not good enough for their child. Most parents are against it. You can't blame them. They had certain dreams for their child, they had a vision — there were things they hoped he would do and he didn't meet their expectations . . . Parents want their child to have another life. They want him to go to school. They want him to become prosperous. They want him to get married. They

want him to have a family. They want him to
have a home and two cars in the garage."

She went on to describe the stereotypes and fears that parents
are confronted with when they first find out about their adult-
child's choice to live an alternative lifestyle:

"To them, their child joined a commune. To
them it's weird. To them it's a cult. Unfortunately, they group all the cults together. They
take all forms of alternative lifestyles and make
them one cult. To them it's a terrible word —
they hear about the murders, the fires, the people
that are mistreated — it sounds terrible. They
don't stop and realize that every group is different, that there are many groups who simply live
together communally and share a certain philosophy — it's like a kibbutz.

Fortunately, many parents will then go to visit
their child. Oftentimes, they see he lives with
normal people and that he's happy. Parents often think that in alternative groups that people go
around like crazy, dressed in crazy things, half-
naked and drunk . . . Instead, they see he's all
right. He's in a sound environment and doing
what he wants."

Charlotte stressed the need for parents to allow their adult-
child the freedom to pursue the lifestyle that he wants to without
arguing with him or otherwise attempting to dissuade him from his
choices.

"It is important for parents not to have a closed-
mind and not to criticize their child for his choices. It's their own child that they're dealing with,

and he's not a child anymore either. He knows
exactly what he's doing. He's a grown person
and he has a mind of his own. He won't become
a member of the stock exchange if this is not his
wish, if this is not what he wants."

She continued to describe how important it can be for an
adult-child to know that his parents understand and support of him.

"Don't blame your child for his choice. Don't
argue with him and say how wrong he is. Try to
understand where he's coming from and what he
is looking for. If you do that and you're supportive, if he doesn't get what he wants from the
community, he'll leave on his own . . . No matter
how much he believes in what he is doing, he
wants his parents to believe in him and be proud
of him."

According to Charlotte, a parent begins to accept her adult-
child's choice when she makes the decision that she is not willing
to lose her adult-child over the issue of how he chooses to live his
life. She reflected:

"Parents start to cooperate when they see they
can't do anything else. Those who don't cooperate lose their child. Parents should never neglect
their child and say to him, 'If you joined a commune that's your fault and stay there!' They
don't need to bless him for doing it, but they
can't pick him up and say, 'We don't want you
to be here. Come home with us.' The way I see
it, if you can't beat them, join them. Parents
don't have to join the commune, but they should
go and see their child, see how he lives."

Charlotte went on to explain that the other thing that prompts a parent to accept her adult-child, even when she doesn't agree with his choices, is her love for him.

> "A parent's willingness to accept her child depends on how much she loves him. It depends on how much the child means to her. If the child means so much to her that no matter how she feels about his lifestyle she doesn't want to loose him, then she has to accept him. Some parents will never be able to accept their child's choices deeply, but on the surface they have to soften up and give a little. If you expect to get a little, you have to give a little. That's what the casinos learned — if you want to get the money from the people, you have to give them a little every once in awhile.
>
> If parents want to have a relationship with their child, they have to be willing to say to him, 'If this is what you really want and if you feel that you're happy here, that's O.K. by me, and if you ever need me, I'm available.' At heart, they may be sick, but if they want their child they have to do this."

As for herself, Charlotte has learned to recognize what is important to her in her relationship to her son, and in doing so has come to recognize the value that his choices have brought to him.

> "He's accepted by people, intelligent people, that's the main thing. He's got a wonderful mind and he's using it — what else can you expect? This is what he wants to do. This is what makes him happy. He doesn't smoke, he doesn't drink, he doesn't take drugs. If he's happy, I'm also happy."

Charlotte has furthermore discovered that she does not need to understand all the specifics of her son's lifestyle in order to accept him and to respect his choices. She explained:

> "A parent doesn't have to understand the philosophy of her child's lifestyle, but she should realize why she doesn't understand it. I don't understand what my son teaches because I don't have to understand it, but it doesn't mean I don't accept it. Even though I don't know exactly what it is all about, I feel perfectly at ease going to the ashram (spiritual community) and staying for the gatherings. As a matter of fact, I like it. I look forward to visiting."

As a result of the degree to which she is able to accept him, Charlotte feels confident in her interactions with friends and relatives around her son's lifestyle — whether or not she decides to speak with them about it. She shares a story about the way in which some of her relatives, who initially didn't want to discuss her son's lifestyle with her, eventually came into an attitude of enthusiasm and acceptance of both her son and the community he created:

> "I have relatives that think that it's a terrible thing to have a guru for a son. They feel sorry for me and assume it is better not to talk about it — they think that if they do not mention it, it will somehow go away. It is actually them who have the difficulty with it, but for a long time I didn't talk about it because they would become so uncomfortable.
>
> Eventually, I invited some of them to come along with me for a visit. They were delighted by what they found. They had no idea what it

was. They didn't know so many people could live together. Everyone sat on the floor together for a big dinner because they didn't have enough tables, and they couldn't believe that one hundred people could have dinner on the floor and be smiling, talking and enjoying themselves. They couldn't get over the way that people were working and being productive. They had this idea that everybody would be running around in rags. They were so happy to be there.

We went to a talk my son gave, and at one point, one of them asked me if I knew what he talking about. 'No,' I told him, ' I don't understand anything.' And I didn't. I don't have to understand."

Charlotte concluded with a discussion of the way in which, when a parent is proud of, and pleased with her adult-child's choice of lifestyle, those around her feel this and often share in her enthusiasm as well. She illustrated this point by a story of the surprise and interest that a group of her peers expressed when she told them about her son's lifestyle:

"I go to elder hostels. In the evenings the women sit in groups and talk. People talk about their children. One has two sons who are big lawyers and make a lot of money. The next has two doctors. The next has a daughter who is a professor.

'Do you have any children?' a woman asked me one night.

'Yes,' I responded, 'I have one son.'

'What does he do?' she wanted to know. I told her that he was a spiritual leader.

'Oh, he's a rabbi?' she questioned.

'No,' I said, 'He's a guru.'

Silence went around the table. They looked at me as if I came from another planet. 'How does a Jewish mother have a son who is a guru?' they wanted to know.

I told them that this is what he had chosen to do and that I accepted it. They became fascinated. They were so interested that whenever they could they would come and ask me, 'Exactly what does he do?' 'What is a guru?' 'What's it like to be his mother?'

They wanted to know if I ever see him and I told them that of course I do. 'What do you do about his religion?' they questioned further.

'I don't take it on for myself,' I told them, 'But I respect it.' That was my reply and it's the truth."

Bibliography

Arrien, Angeles. *The Four-Fold Way*. San Francisco, CA: Harper Collins, 1993.

Baldwin, Christina. *One To One: Self-Understanding through Journal Writing*. New York: M. Evans, 1977.

Beattie, Melody. *Codependent No More*. Center City, MN: Hazelden Educational Materials, 1987.

Berends, Polly Berrien. *Whole Child / Whole Parent (A Spiritual and Practical Guide to Parenthood)*. New York: Harper & Row, 1983.

Bettelheim, Bruno. *A Good Enough Parent*. New York: Alfred A. Knopf, 1987.

Bloomfield, Harold H. *Making Peace With Your Parents*. New York: Random House, 1983.

Bolton, Robert. *People Skills: How to Assert Yourself, Listen to Others, and Resolve Conflicts*. New York: Simon and Schuster, 1979.

Bowlby, John. *Separation: Anxiety and Anger*. New York: Basic Books, 1973.

Bradshaw, John. *Healing The Shame that Binds You*. Deerfield Beach, FL: Health Communications, 1988.

Bradshaw, John. *On the Family: A Revolutionary Way of*

Self-Discovery. Pompano Beach, FL: Health Communications, 1988.

Bridges, Bill. *Transitions: Making Sense of Life's Changes.* Reading, MA: Addison-Wesley, 1980.

Buscaglia, Leo. *Born for Love: Reflections on Loving.* New York: Fawcett Columbine, 1992.

Capacchione, Lucia. *The Creative Journal: The Art of Finding Yourself.* North Hollywood, CA: Newcastle Publishing Co., Inc., 1989.

Briggs, D.C. *Embracing Life: Growing Through Love and Loss.* New York: Doubleday, 1985.

Fromm, Erich. *The Art of Loving.* New York: Harper & Row, 1965.

Gravitz, Herbert L. and Julie D. Bowden. *Guide To Recovery: A Book For Adult Children Of Alcoholics.* Holmes Beach, FL: Learning Publications, 1985.

Holt, John. *Escape From Childhood: The Needs and Rights of Children.* New York: Ballantine Books, 1974.

James, John, and Frank Cherry. *The Grief Recovery Handbook: A Step-by-Step Program for Moving Beyond Loss.* New York: HarperPerennial, 1988.

Jampolsky, Gerald G. *Love is Letting Go of Fear.* New York: Bantam Books, 1979.

Jampolsky, Gerald G. *One Person CAN Make A Difference.* New York: Bantam Books, 1990.

Jen, Erica, Lalitha Thomas and Regina Sara Ryan. *Everywoman's Book of Common Wisdom.* Prescott, AZ: Hohm Press, 1995.

Laing, R.D. *The Politics of the Family.* New York: Vintage

Books, 1972.

Liedloff, Jean. *The Continuum Concept.* Reading, MA: Addison-Wesley Publishing Co., 1975.

Lozowick, Lee. *The Alchemy of Transformation.* Prescott, AZ: Hohm Press, 1996.

Miller, Alice. *Banished Knowledge: Facing Childhood Injuries.* New York: Bantam Publishing, 1990.

Paul, Dr. Jordan, and Dr. Margaret Paul with Bonnie B. Hesse. *Do I Have to Give Up Me to Be Loved By You?* Minneapolis, MN: CompCare, 1983.

Pearce, Joseph Chilton. *Magical Child: Rediscovering Natures Plan for Our Children.* New York: Bantam Books, 1986.

Peck, M. Scott. *A Different Drum: Community Making and Peace.* New York: Simon & Schuster, 1987.

Peck, M. Scott., *The Road Less Traveled: A New Psychology of Love, Traditional Values, and Spiritual Growth.* New York: Simon & Schuster, 1978.

Rogers, Carl. *On Becoming a Person.* Boston, MA: Houghton Mifflin, 1961.

Satir, Virginia. *Peoplemaking.* Palo Alto, CA: Science & Behavior Books, 1972.

Stearns, Ann Kaiser. *Living Through Personal Crisis.* New York: Ballantine Books, 1984.

Stettbacher, J. Konrad. *Making Sense of Suffering.* New York: Penguin Books, 1991.

Stinnett, Nick, and John DeFrain. *Secrets of Strong Families.* New York: Berkeley Books, 1985.

Stone, Hal, and Sidra Stone. *Embracing Ourselves: The Voice Dialogue Manual.* Novato, CA: Nataraj, 1989.

Viorst, Judith. *Necessary Losses: The Loves, Illusions, Dependencies and Impossible Expectations That All of Us Have to Give Up in Order to Grow.* New York: Simon & Schuster, 1986.

Woodman, Marion. *Leaving My Father's House.* Boston: Shambhala; Distributed in the U.S. by Random House, 1992.

ADDITIONAL TITLES OF INTEREST FROM HOHM PRESS

THE JUMP INTO LIFE: Moving Beyond Fear
by Arnaud Desjardins
Foreword by Richard Moss, M.D.

"Say *Yes* to life," the author continually invites in this welcome guide-book to the spiritual path. For anyone who has ever felt oppressed by the life-negative seriousness of religion, this book is a timely antidote. In language that translates the complex to the obvious, Desjardins applies his simple teaching of happiness and gratitude to a broad range of weighty topics, including sexuality and intimate relationships, structuring an "inner life," the relief of suffering, and overcoming fear.
Paper, 217 pages, $12.95, ISBN: 0-934252-42-4

EVERYWOMAN'S BOOK OF COMMON WISDOM
by Erica Jen, Lalitha Thomas and Regina Sara Ryan

This wise and fresh book of aphorisms is written by women for women (or anyone else who wants to eavesdrop on women's advice to their friends and sisters). From the paradoxical ("It's OK to hate, just be kind to others") and the satirical ("I'd rather be a woman than be right,"), to the challenging ("If you find a good man, be a good woman") and the inspirational ("Keep on giving yourself a chance"!) this little volume covers a full spectrum of emotions, moods, and topics in a straightfor-ward way that will delight and intrigue female readers (and their male friends or partners) of all ages.
Paper, 134 pages, $6.95, ISBN: 0-934252-52-1

ENNEATYPES IN PSYCHOTHERAPY
by Claudio Naranjo, M.D.

Dr.Claudio Naranjo —world-renowned Gestalt therapist, educator and Enneagram pioneer—conducted the First International Symposium on the Personality Enneagrams in Pueblo Acantilado, Spain in December 1993. This book derives from this conference and reflects the direct ex-perience and lively testimony of notable representatives of a variety of

therapeutic disciplines — including: psychoanalysis, Gestalt, Transactional Analysis, bodywork, and others. Each writer describes how the Enneagram holds invaluable keys to understanding personality and its special relevance to those whose task is helping others.
Paper, 160 pages, $14.95, ISBN: 0-934252-47-5

THE ALCHEMY OF TRANSFORMATION
by Lee Lozowick
Foreword by: Claudio Naranjo, M.D.

A concise and straightforward overview of the principles of spiritual life as developed and taught by Lee Lozowick (author of *The Alchemy of Love and Sex,* Hohm Press, 1995) for the past twenty years. Subjects of use to seekers and serious students of any spiritual tradition. A radical, elegant and irreverent approach to the possibility of change from ego-centeredness to God-centeredness—the ultimate human transformation .
Paper, 185 pages; $14.95; ISBN: 0-934252-62-9

THE ART OF TOUCH: A Massage Manual For Young People
by Chia Martin

Provides young people (ages 9 and up) with a simple, step-by-step method for learning massage techniques to use on themselves and others for health, pain relief and increased self-esteem. Encourages a young person to respect his/her own body and the bodies of others.

Photographs clearly demonstrate proper hand placement and capture the mood of gentleness and playfulness which the author encourages throughout the text. Adults will also enjoy reading about and practicing these techniques.
Paper, 60 pages, 92 photographs, $15.95, ISBN: 0-934252-57-2

Additional Titles of Interest from Hohm Press

COLOR YOUR HAIR RED
A Story of One Woman's Liberation
by Polly Döge

A dream-like reflection upon the author's life and times, the book follows the threads of several realities weaving together a raw, sensitive and fascinating chronicle of one woman's liberation. Unembarrassed prose and sure dialogue venture into the areas of sexuality, relationships, the creative process, the traumas of childbirth in the technological age and the secrets that women know about men, and about themselves.
Paper, 128 pages; $11.95; ISBN:0-934252-59-9

THE WAY OF POWER
by Red Hawk

Nominated for the 1992 Pulitzer Prize in poetry for his previous collection, *The Sioux Dog Dance*, Red Hawk here delivers another substantial menu of poems. His powerful and exquisite selections deal with the many blatant and disguised abuses of power enacted everyday by individuals and governments. Red Hawk writes with passion and tenderness of the Earth, of women, of dispossessed people everywhere and of children.

"Red Hawk is a true poet whose work has strong, credible feelings and excellent timing." —Richard Wilbur, Pulitzer Prize winner, 1957 & 1989; Poet Laureate of the US, 1987-88.
Paper, 96 pages; $10.00; ISBN: 0-934252-64-5

To order: 1-800-381-2700

Hohm Press
P.O. Box 2501
Prescott, Arizona 86302

Hohm Press
P.O. Box 2501
Prescott, Arizona 86302

HOHM PRESS publishes fine spiritual literature as well as works
in the fields of health, poetry, and children's books. If this book
was of interest to you we will be happy to send you a catalog.

Name _____

Street or box number _____

City _____

State _____   Zip _____

HOHM PRESS publishes fine spiritual literature as well as works
in the fields of health, poetry, and children's books. If this book
was of interest to you we will be happy to send you a catalog.

Name _____

Street or box number _____

City _____

State _____   Zip _____